Beyond Futility

Also by David Allan Hubbard

WITH BANDS OF LOVE: Lessons from the Book of Hosea
PSALMS FOR ALL SEASONS
MORE PSALMS FOR ALL SEASONS

Beyond Futility

Messages of Hope from the Book of Ecclesiastes

by

David Allan Hubbard

William B. Eerdmans Publishing Company

Copyright © 1976 by
William B. Eerdmans Publishing Company
255 Jefferson Ave. SE, Grand Rapids, Michigan 49502
All rights reserved
Printed in the United States of America

Library of Congress Cataloging in Publication Data

Hubbard, David Allan.
    Beyond futility.

    "First used as Bible studies on the Joyful Sound,
an international radio broadcast by the Fuller Evangelistic
Association."
    1. Bible. O. T. Ecclesiastes—Criticism, inter-
pretation, etc. I. The Joyful Sound. II. Title.
BS1475.2.H82   223′.8′06   76–2196
ISBN 0–8028–1650–9

Table of Contents

Preface

The chapters in this book were first used as Bible studies on The Joyful Sound, an international radio broadcast sponsored by the Fuller Evangelistic Association. Some of the material was also used at the Christian Reformed Ministers' Institute, Grand Rapids, Michigan, in June, 1975. The editing and typing were done by my wife Ruth. She has added measurably to whatever conciseness and clarity the book possesses.

Biblical quotations are from the Revised Standard Version, copyright 1946 and 1952, and are used by permission of the Division of Christian Education of the National Council of Churches of Christ.

Introduction

Anyone to whom the book of Ecclesiastes is not a puzzle has not yet read it. Through the centuries, preachers and scholars, teachers and lay persons, have wondered at its purpose and questioned its meaning.

The intent of this little book is to make some contribution to the unraveling of Ecclesiastes' puzzle. To do so, one has to make some comments on the setting and background of the book.

Ecclesiastes is, of course, a title, not a name. It is the Greek equivalent of the Hebrew word *Qoheleth* (or Koheleth) which seems to indicate an officer of the congregation (Hebrew: *Qahal*; Greek: *Ekklesia*). Whether the office held is that of a Convener, who calls the congregation together, or a Preacher, who addresses the congregation, we cannot tell. The popular translation, Preacher, will serve us adequately, as long as we do not confuse the Old Testament wise man who used the title, with a New Testament herald of God's saving grace in Jesus Christ. The skeptical bent of Ecclesiastes has prompted some to call him a Professor, and that translation, too, has some merit, if we do not project upon the scene the accoutrements of a modern university.

That Ecclesiastes was a wise man, we cannot doubt. His use of personal illustration, his warnings against false values, his familiarity with the proverbs of the day—all these mark him as a practitioner of wisdom, the art of explaining reality on the basis of observing the way nature and human experience work. It was probably a student of the Preacher who gave us a clear description of the wise man's work:

> Besides being wise, the Preacher also taught the people knowledge, weighing and studying and arranging proverbs with great care. The Preacher sought to find pleasing words, and uprightly he wrote words of truth. (Eccl. 12:9–10)

When the Preacher lived is hard to determine. The style of Hebrew suggests a date after the Exile. Perhaps somewhere between 450 and 250 B.C. is as close as we can come. Placing the book in this period suggests that Solomon, who lived in the tenth century before Christ, was not the final author. In fact Solomon's name is not mentioned in the book, where the speaker is identified as "son (or descendant) of David, King in Jerusalem" (Eccl. 1:1; cf. 1:12). The identification is deliberately vague and does not occur after chapter two. The author's purpose, apparently, was not to claim to be Solomon but rather to use Solomon's experiences as the backdrop for his argument. How better could a wise man illustrate the limits of wisdom, pleasure, prestige, wealth, and achievement than to cite Solomon's experiences? In a later setting, then, the younger wise man donned Solomon's robes to explore the deficiencies of a way of life based on Solomonic values.

What we can say about the setting is that the times seem to have been hard. Not financially hard, as though money were tight; and not militarily hard, as though invasion were imminent. But spiritually and emotionally hard. Much of the vitality has been drained from the faith of the people. Their hope in God's presence with them has been jaded; their religious beliefs have been narrowed to formal ritual, carelessly practiced. Commercial success seemed to have snared their attention, by a preoccupation with profits, material goods, and luxurious living.

When they did trust God, they tended to bleed the mystery out of his ways and leave them limply predictable. They had overlearned the lessons of traditional wisdom—that God would reward with material blessings those who did right.

A God who is completely predictable would cease to be God. He would be subject to the manipulations of mere mortals and would thus be inferior to them. Whatever else God must be, he must be free— free to work his will, free to achieve his purposes, free to deal with human frailty and failure, free to lavish his grace upon those who do not deserve it.

Like Job, Ecclesiastes was written to make clear that God is free, free to be mysterious, free not to work on our terms, free to work only on his own terms. If the Preacher pushed his arguments about the vanity, the emptiness, the futility of his countrymen's ways, it was to make his crucial points: God is not to be taken for granted; human values are not ultimately dependable; our best response is to make the most of what God has given us in our work, our families, and our enjoyment of his gifts. If Ecclesiastes fell short of both the ringing faith of the Hebrew prophets and the resounding hope of the Christian gospel, it is because he lived in different times. But for those times, and for ours, he served God's purposes well. He laid bare both the foolish idolatries and the hollow beliefs of his generation. In so doing he prepared the way for the greater Wise Man, whose person revealed to the human family the fullness both of God's wisdom and God's freedom.

In each chapter I have tried to show how the Preacher challenged the superficial attitudes and distorted values of his fellows. With scathing criticism he exposed the dry rot in the platform on which their lives were built. What he proposed as a substitute support was realistic, if only temporary. Surely it was better to enjoy God's ordinary gifts daily than to bank on counterfeit capital like pleasure, prestige, or wealth.

But a still better foundation was needed. If the older one had collapsed, imperfectly based on the teachings of the older wise men (like those whose sayings are preserved in our biblical book of Proverbs), and if the later foundation, based on the realism of the Preacher, was only temporary, then the ground was cleared for the only Foundation which has both adequacy and permanence—Jesus Christ our Lord.

This movement from poorer foundation to better foundation to only Foundation—from the older to the newer to the best wisdom—I have tried to trace in each chapter. In so doing I have wanted to appreciate both the limitations and the contributions of Ecclesiastes. I have great respect for the Preacher's insights. A happy choice of God's providence it was that preserved his little book as part of the Scriptures which God's people cherish and obey. Though his lessons are not the ultimate ones, they are utterly necessary to reveal our human foolishness and to protect us from it. Wise indeed is the Holy Spirit of God who opened the wise man's eyes to life's futilities and pointed them to a better Way beyond.

1 / Beyond Futility
   —to Meaning

Ecclesiastes 1:1–11

Their question stopped me in my tracks. They had not put it to me that way before. Perhaps it was a drawn look on my face, perhaps it was the fact that I was five minutes late to class that prompted the students to ask me the question. Students I call them, though they were actually pastors—friends and colleagues of mine in ministry—who were taking a special course at the Seminary to sharpen their skills and expand their understanding.

They sensed that I was troubled, and they gave me opportunity to talk about it with the question, "Had a good day?" A good day? I could have wept. I had just concluded an extended phone call that seemed to unravel a project I had been working on for three months. Just when I thought I had the whole pattern put together, it fell apart at my feet.

A good day? they had asked. And with moist eyes I shared the deep futility that I was feeling.

Futile days we can expect from time to time. Some of what we plan will miscarry. Paths that look promising will peter out and force us to backtrack.

Pillars that we lean on will collapse and send our hopes tumbling down on us.

When sickness strikes or financial reverses hit, futile days may stretch into empty weeks or months. There have been times when we heaved huge sighs as we ripped December's page from the calendar and welcomed a new year that offered better days than the old.

Days, weeks, months, even years can be tinged with or stamped by futility. Life's complexion is scarcely ever totally free of blemishes. It does have its bleak side. But the Preacher in the book of Ecclesiastes viewed it in consistently dark tones. His opinion was not that life is basically and usually good—with occasionally painful exceptions. To the contrary, he announced, life can only be labeled good when you do not look closely at it.

A careful analysis of life's circumstances and human experiences indicates a deep-seated futility. This futility is akin to irony, because it is full of surprises. We find it where we least expect it. Values that we treasure prove false; efforts that should succeed come to failure; pleasures that should satisfy increase our thirst. Ironic futility, futile irony—that is the color of life as seen through the Preacher's eyes.

Throughout his twelve chapters he argued one main point—it is incredibly difficult for us as human beings to move *beyond futility*. This is the meaning of the famous pronouncement with which his book begins:

> Vanity of vanities, says the Preacher,
> vanity of vanities! All is vanity. (Eccl. 1:2)

Strong language the Preacher used. *Everything* is

empty, hollow, futile. Life is not what it seems, not what we want it to be. Not only is everything vanity, but it is the vainest kind of vanity, the most futile brand of futility. The expression conveys a superlative quality. As "Song of Songs" means the finest song and as "King of kings" points to the greatest King, so "vanity of vanities" means that life is as empty as possible; it is marked by the worst sort of futility.

The strong words of the Preacher were prompted by his disagreement with his fellow wise men. Their teachings were full of promises about the possibilities of wealth, security, happiness, and blessing. Koheleth, as the Preacher is called in Hebrew, objected. He thought that the other teachers were promising more than life could produce. They were misleading people with the unrealistic dreams that they painted. They failed at two points in particular: they tried to predict God's ways without due respect for the mysteries involved; and they ignored the fact of death which cut short their plans and left their wealth to others.

In argument after argument the Preacher tried to expose the blind spots in the teachings of these traditional wise men and to discourage his own pupils from building their lives on values doomed to collapse. To make his points he deliberately attacked the beliefs and opinions of his society. Ideas they had cherished and customs they had practiced he exploded as vapid, vanishing, and vain.

Futility is the brush with which he tarred their highest hopes, their broadest dreams, their deepest convictions. Try as they would they could not get beyond this futility in their attitude toward work, their relationship to creation, their sense of history.

Work, creation, history—these concepts take us to the heart of life as the men and women of Israel viewed it. They valued work as a key to success; they respected creation as the handiwork of God; they honored history as the arena where God had entered into covenant with them and where God would fulfill all his promises to them. The Preacher's criticisms, then, were neither casual nor superficial; they were serious and penetrating. They probed to the core of what his countrymen believed in these crucial aspects of their world view.

Beyond Futility—to Profit in Work

No profit in work—that was Koheleth's first proof of his thesis that everything in life is stamped with vanity:

> What does a man gain by all the toil
>   at which he toils under the sun?
> A generation goes, and a generation comes,
>   but the earth remains for ever. (Eccl. 1:3–4)

Work does not really make a difference in life. We do not fully subdue the earth, despite all our trying. We till and rake and plant and water; we build our dams, develop our lakes, reshape the contours of our land— but in the long run the earth wins the struggle. It wears us down—generation after generation—while we rarely improve it and sometimes despoil it.

Here the Preacher hit the opinions of his fellow wise men full in the face. For centuries they had been extolling the profits to be found in hard work. It was a key to personal success and to national stability. They taught generations of disciples with words like these:

> He who tills his land will have plenty of bread,
>> but he who follows worthless pursuits has no
>>> sense. (Prov. 12:11)

Work, not idleness, is what pays off—and work, not talk, does the same, according to the other teachers:

> In all toil there is profit,
>> but mere talk tends only to want. (Prov. 14:23)

No gain in toil, the Preacher concluded. "In all toil there is profit," the wise men had taught. What they prized, he deemed futile; what they valued he called vain.

And we can see why. Much of our toil is monotonous routine never really accomplished. You think you have all the dishes washed and from a bedroom or a bathroom there appears, as from a ghost, another dirty glass. And even when all the dishes are washed, it is only a few hours until they demand washing again.

So much of our work is cyclical, and so much of it futile. We shape plans that collapse; we pinch out savings that shrink; we toil for promotions that others get; we leave our goods to governments or heirs that squander them.

Yet we have to go on working. Even the discouraged Professor, as we might call Koheleth, did not advocate giving up work and waiting for death to come. But how can we move beyond its apparent futility? How can we find true, lasting profit in our labors?

In the deeds and words of a later, greater Wise Man, we find our answers. Part of the gospel's good news is that our work—even though routine and tedious—need not be futile. Jesus had, as part of his mission, the purpose of taking us beyond futility to profit in our work.

Perhaps that is why he came as a carpenter. Tools he knew how to handle. Orders from customers he had to fill. Wood and iron were the stuff he worked with. His knuckles felt knicks and his fingers knew blisters. The Son of God entered our human labor crew. Shoulder to shoulder he toiled with the rest of us. Doing God's will entailed doing menial work. He did it with diligence and delight.

And he linked his daily work to the work beyond work—the doing of the Father's will and the trusting of the Father's power. He urged his hearers to engage in this same spiritual work: "Do not labor for the food which perishes, but for the food which endures to eternal life . . ." (John 6:27). And more positively, "This is the work of God, that you believe in him whom he has sent" (John 6:29).

To trust Jesus for rescue from our sins, to trust Jesus for guidance for our lives, to trust Jesus for power in our service—that is the work of God, the work beyond work, the true work, in which all our work becomes profitable. Futility in work? That verdict is now passé. Better news about work is at hand. Jesus has brought it.

Beyond Futility — to Joy in Creation

If the Preacher's outlook on work seemed jaded, listen to what he thought about creation:

> The sun rises and the sun goes down,
>   and hastens to the place where it rises.
> The wind blows to the south,
>   and goes round to the north;

> round and round goes the wind,
>> and on its circuits the wind returns.
> All streams run to the sea,
>> but the sea is not full;
> to the place where the streams flow,
>> there they flow again. (Eccl. 1:5–7)

Symbols of monotony they have become—the sun, the wind, the streams. Their course is set; their path is determined; their pace is fixed. No human effort can make them different; no human joy can be extracted from them.

What a different picture this is from what we usually find in Scripture. To Koheleth the sun spoke of searing dreariness, but the Psalmist saw it as a strong man that "runs its course with joy" (Ps. 19:5). To Koheleth the wind was a sign of whimsical monotony, but the Psalmist knew it as a messenger of God (Ps. 104:4). To Koheleth, the streams were symptoms of futility spending themselves in the sea but never filling it, yet the Psalmist viewed them as a reminder of the "river whose streams make glad the city of God" (Ps. 46:4).

A confusing picture this is. Do we sigh over creation's monotony or do we celebrate creation's vitality? Is nature a friend or an enemy?

Again, Jesus had good news for us. His very birth in our kind of manger and in our kind of flesh told us about creation—the place where God's love and care are at work. Not a menace to our welfare but a means of our sustenance, not evidence of life's dreariness but witness to God's glory—that is creation as Jesus treated it. Spiritual stories from seed and soil, fatherly care of sparrows and lilies, kindly transformation of water to wine at a wedding—Jesus, the Lord of creation, was at home in what he had made. And we can be too.

But his miracles sometimes took us to the creation beyond creation: the new creation, the wonder of the coming age. As Lord of the sea, he subdued creation's turbulence. As Lord of disease, he healed creation's woundedness. As Lord of demons, he defeated creation's enemies. As Lord of death, he determined creation's outcome. And by his resurrection he has led his people into the realm of the new creation where God's will is fully done and God's glory fully seen. Futility in creation? That pronouncement has been cancelled. Better news about creation is here. Jesus has proclaimed it.

Beyond Futility—to Direction in History

History, as well as work and creation, was tarred with the Preacher's brush of futility. Two phrases betray that dark smear: ". . . there is nothing new under the sun" and "there is no remembrance of former things . . ." (Eccl. 1:9,11).

How sharply that opinion clashed with the words of Israel's prophets. They looked forward to new things God was yet to do and urged their people to sing new songs as the new things happened. They also encouraged their followers to remember what God had done for them in their history past and to live in the light of those deeds.

Nothing new? Is history headed nowhere? Nothing worth remembering? Is history a stagnant heap of oblivion?

No, is the answer which Jesus' good news shouts to those questions. History still has its surprises, and Jesus' appearance in human flesh was one of them. New covenants, new commandments, new persons, new heavens and new earth are all yet to come. Jesus entered our history to teach us to remember and to hope. He pointed to a past worth recalling in his death and resurrection; he depicted a future worth anticipating in his church and his return.

Our history he entered and rewrote with his love and grace. And to the history beyond he called us, the history of a Kingdom without end. Futility in history? That opinion has been nullified. Better news about history has arrived. Jesus has demonstrated it.

Futile days and futile weeks we may have, where life loses its glue and turns leaky at the seams. But a futile life will not be our lot. Christ's news is too good to let that happen. Life is filled with meaning because he is making all things new—beginning with us.

2 / Beyond Futility
—to Wisdom

Ecclesiastes 1:12–18

I hated to dampen their sparkling spirits, but I had to help them face reality. Year after year I went through the experience. It was during the time I served as a teacher at Westmont College in Santa Barbara. Each Fall I had the privilege of addressing the entering class, eager as they were to savor their new experience, zealous as they were to pursue their course of learning.

I hated to weigh down their buoyant minds, but I had to help them see what they were in for. What do you want to get out of college? I would ask them. Spiritual inspiration? Great! I am all for it, but if that is your main goal you should go to summer conferences and deeper life retreats. What do you seek in college? Fun? Good times? Friendships? Recreation? Fine! I would answer, but you would find all of them in your local country club—and for far less money. What is it you are looking for in these halls of learning? Information? Facts? Knowledge? Excellent! I heartily approved, but would you not do better to buy a comprehensive encyclopedia and memorize its data in the comfort of your own home?

I could not guarantee that the bright, bubbly men and women in the freshman class would gain spiritual inspiration, wholesome recreation, or useful information, though I hoped and prayed that their cup would be filled with these daily. What I did guarantee was something quite different, something totally unexpected. You can be sure that one thing will happen to you, if your college education really takes: your capacity for suffering will increase.

Here I had the wise Preacher, Ecclesiastes (whom the Jews call Koheleth), on my side. He knew full well the pains inherent in the pursuit of wisdom:

> For in much wisdom is much vexation,
>   and he who increases knowledge increases
>   sorrow. (Eccl. 1:18)

With a jolt these words must have hit Koheleth's students. The contradiction between this view of wisdom and what was normally taught was arresting, to say the least. We do not have to leaf far in the book of Proverbs to feel the sting of this contradiction:

> Happy is the man who finds wisdom,
>   and the man who gets understanding,
> for the gain from it is better than gain from silver
>   and its profit better than gold.
> She is more precious than jewels,
>   and nothing you desire can compare with her.
> Long life is in her right hand;
>   in her left hand are riches and honor.
> Her ways are ways of pleasantness,
>   and all her paths are peace.
> She is a tree of life to those who lay hold of her;
>   those who hold her fast are called happy. (Prov.
>   3:13–18)

The dividends promised from an investment in wisdom are lavish indeed: long life, riches, honor, pleasantness, peace, happiness. No one can vote against any item in that list. It is more than we dare ask from the most generous Santa Claus in life.

What the Preacher has said in his own abrupt, almost gruff, way is that there is another side to wisdom that coats it with irony. Far from producing all that happiness and prosperity, wisdom has several handicaps with which those who quest after it must reckon.

To make his point dramatically the Preacher donned the royal robes of Solomon and put himself into the experience of the great king. He did this for two reasons. First, Solomon's wisdom was celebrated. If any person had enough wisdom to assure him blessing and happiness, Solomon did. His prayer to God had been:

> "give thy servant therefore an understanding mind to govern thy people, that I may discern between good and evil; for who is able to govern this thy great people?" (1 Kings 3:9)

God's answer was a resounding "Yes" to Solomon's request:

> "behold, I now do according to your word. Behold I give you a wise and discerning mind, so that none like you has been before you and none like you shall arise after you." (1 Kings 3:12)

Koheleth's second reason for assuming the role of Solomon in this passage is that the people who most needed the message were ardent disciples of Solomon. They esteemed him as the founder and patron of their

24

whole movement. He it was whose "wisdom surpassed the wisdom of all the people of the east, and all the wisdom of Egypt." He it was who "uttered three thousand proverbs" and whose "songs were a thousand and five" (1 Kings 4:30,32).

The Wise Preacher's Conclusion

So Koheleth began to speak as though he were Solomon to prove his case that wisdom was not the solution to all human problems, as the other, older wise men had sometimes implied:

> I the Preacher have been king over Israel in Jerusalem. And I applied my mind to seek and to search out by wisdom all that is done under heaven. (Eccl. 1:12,13)

Investigating the data of life was the normal task of a wise man. Habits of animals, patterns of plants, customs of tribes, families, and persons—these were carefully analyzed so that general principles or rules for human behavior could be learned and taught. Again it was Solomon who had pioneered this path by probing curiously into every area of life:

> He spoke of trees, from the cedar that is in Lebanon to the hyssop that grows out of the wall; he spoke also of beasts, and of birds, and of reptiles, and of fish. (1 Kings 4:33)

As psychologists, sociologists, and anthropologists today look over the shoulders of biologists and zoologists to gain insights into human behavior, so the whole range of creation and experience was the laboratory for Koheleth and his colleagues. These fellow wise men understood the Preacher's methods of investigation. They were appalled at his conclusions:

> it is an unhappy business that God has given to the sons of men to be busy with. I have seen everything that is done under the sun; and behold, all is vanity and a striving after wind. (Eccl. 1:13–14)

Not the lack of wisdom, but the presence of wisdom was what bothered Koheleth. He found what he had sought and it proved futile. Far from being the solid rock on which a sound life could be built, wisdom was as insubstantial as a vapor, as undependable as a breeze. Reach to clutch it, and the movement of your hand blows it away. Think you have it, and it seeps between your fingers.

This dreadful conclusion about the limitations of wisdom was based on two reasons. First, *wisdom cannot change reality*. Much of what is wrong with life is not wisdom's fault; it is just the way things are. Full of injustice, stamped by suffering, plagued by weakness, terrorized by crime, life has so much wrong about it that wisdom stands by powerless to do more than observe. Think of the massive problems that confront our huge cities: treasuries on the edge of bankruptcy, unemployment at alarming levels, education perplexed about its directions, crime rates soaring to eagle heights. Wisdom is much better able to analyze the trends than it is to prescribe the solutions. Our wise man must have had this in mind when he wrote these puzzling words:

> What is crooked cannot be made straight,
>   and what is lacking cannot be numbered. (Eccl. 1:15)

Wisdom may finger the problem but it cannot straighten out what is crooked or add to what is lacking. Wisdom cannot change reality.

But *wisdom can increase sorrow.* That was Koheleth's second reason for doubting the value which the other wise man had credited to wisdom. With life as crooked and as lacking as it is, wisdom only calls attention to the sour notes; it cannot bring the singing into tune. If the choir cannot sing the notes, if the rhythm and the pitch are faulty, if the words are pronounced sloppily, it is better for the people listening not to be trained musicians. If they are, they will agree with the Preacher:

> For in much wisdom is much vexation,
> and he who increases knowledge increases
> sorrow. (Eccl. 1:18)

The wiser they are in things musical, the more a bad performance will pain them.

This is what I tried to put across to those fledgling students eager to flex their wings in college. Wisdom and knowledge in themselves will not satisfy. By exposing life's sorry sides, they may actually increase our pain.

The Wise Savior's Commitment

As doubtful as the Preacher was about attaching too much importance to wisdom, he did not suggest that it was better to be ignorant or foolish. In fact, he used keen wisdom to show us what wisdom could not do. He proved how much he valued wisdom while he demonstrated the limits to its value. He pointed out its substance by the wisdom he used to argue for its futility.

And he did us a service. It is easy for us to confuse a wise man with a smart aleck. They are not the same. But he did not take us far enough. It remained for another Wise Man—a Wise Man who was not only a wise Preacher but a wise Savior—to take us beyond the futility of wisdom to its solid core.

More wisdom than Solomon knew was found in Jesus the Christ: for the Queen of Sheba "came from the ends of the earth to hear the wisdom of Solomon, and behold, something greater than Solomon is here" (Matt. 12:42). Through his wisdom we move beyond futility to a true wisdom, a wisdom from above (James 3:17).

Wisdom can change reality—that was part of the startling change that Jesus brought to light. Wisdom as Jesus revealed it was not the product of deep study, but of strong commitment. It was not written on a scroll, but emblazoned on a cross.

The cross with its power of forgiveness, the cross with its wisdom of love can make the crooked things of life straight and can add to what life lacks. What the best of human wisdom could not do, Jesus Christ—the power and wisdom of God—has done (1 Cor. 1:18–25). He has settled our debt to God; he has charted our direction in life; he has sorted out our confused values; he has freed our enslaved spirits.

Reality has been changed. Only God was wise enough to change it. True wisdom was not only Jesus' instruction about right and wrong, but Jesus' commitment—a commitment to death—to make us right where we were wrong.

Wisdom can increase happiness. That was the

other part of the Savior's commitment. The change in our reality has brought a change in our welfare. Hear these assuring words: "He [that is, God] is the source of your life in Christ Jesus, whom God made our wisdom, our righteousness and sanctification and redemption" (1 Cor. 1:30). These are the words that make for happiness—not the long life, honor, wealth, peace, and blessing the older wisdom offered.

These words—righteousness, sanctification, redemption—ring with the notes of relationship. They tell us that God has brought us out of our slavery into his family; he has cleansed us of our pollution and made us fit for his fellowship. We have come to terms with God because of Christ's commitment to us—that is the meaning of happiness, that is the path of wisdom.

3 / Beyond Futility —to Pleasure

Ecclesiastes 2:1–11

A day at the county fair—I suppose that was the dream of all of us as youngsters. With pulses racing, voices rising, and eyes darting, we would push our way through the crowds to our favorite booths. What an array of them to choose from! And what a wealth of wonders those stalls sheltered! Snow cones, candied apples, chocolate fudge, homemade ice cream, cotton candy, deep dish apple pie, long ropes of licorice—these were only a sampling of the delights that beckoned for our attention and bargained for our pennies.

That was just the beginning. The county fair was much more than a massive sweet shop. It was also a vast marketplace of homemade goods. From hand-knit sweaters to patch quilts, from home-canned peaches to farm-churned butter, from carved wood figurines to kiln baked candlesticks, the labors of a thousand hands were on display.

And so was the produce of the fields. From the pens and sheds behind the booths there sounded the chorus of the livestock. Mooing cows, braying donkeys, neighing horses and bleating sheep all blended in a barnyard cantata. But it was not for their music that the animals were on display. It was the richness of the milk, the thickness of the wool, the squareness of the shoulders, the soundness of the legs that the judges inspected. White, red, and, especially, blue ribbons were the praise the ranchers waited for.

At night the air was filled with entertainment—the rhythm of the square dance, the circling lights of the ferris wheel, the crack of the target rifles, and especially the blazing, dazzling radiance of the fireworks. It was an evening worth staying up late for.

A cafeteria of pleasure, an emporium of entertainment, the county fair was—and still is in some places. It offers in the confines of one place and in the span of a few days a summary of our human delight in food, play, competition, and achievement. For small boys and girls of all ages it was the highlight of the year.

The wise Professor who shared his experiences and his viewpoints in the book of Ecclesiastes would have enjoyed the county fair. He would have understood the intrigue with which a fair can put its noose around our hearts and bind us to its attractions.

Pleasure was part of the agenda he set for himself; it was a key course in his curriculum to understand life. After he tested wisdom and found out that its contribution was limited because it had the power to increase human suffering but not the power to change reality, he turned next to pleasure to see what depths of meaning he could find in it. Again he put himself in Solomon's place, mindful that no one else in Israel's long history had greater power, wealth, and leisure to give the search for pleasure its full play.

The Lure of Pleasure

Speaking for Solomon, the Preacher recounted his search:

> I said to myself, "Come now, I will make a test of pleasure; enjoy yourself." (Eccl. 2:1).

Then, as was his custom in this book, he gave his conclusion before he stated his case:

> But behold, this also was vanity. I said of laughter, "It is mad," and of pleasure, "What use is it?" (Eccl. 2:1–2)

Only after he had announced the futile results of his pilgrimage into pleasure, did he take time to rehearse its stages.

We must not let the bluntness of his conclusion—pleasure is empty—blind us to the lure of pleasure. You can be sure that the wise man enjoyed himself a good bit while working toward his negative conclusion.

After all, part of pleasure's lure is that it offers to *heighten our senses*. We are made to enjoy a tender touch, a tasty morsel, a tangy beverage, a graceful figure, a delicate perfume. From the standpoint of our senses, we might conclude that pleasure is what we were made for. The Preacher sought to test that view of life by abandoning himself to pleasure. He gave his senses every chance to thrill and tingle, to stir and soothe. Would he uncover life's full purpose by arousing his sensitivities? He thought it worth a try:

> I searched with my mind how to cheer my body with wine—my mind still guiding me with wisdom—and how to lay hold on folly, till I might

32

see what was good for the sons of men to do under heaven during the few days of their life. (Eccl. 2:3)

The wise man's very language suggested how difficult the human quest for meaning is. The *good* in life—what is really worth going after—was not at all apparent. Therefore, the Preacher had to search diligently. Furthermore, there are severe limitations placed on our humanity: it is lived "under heaven," subject to the terms laid down by God; and one of those terms is that life lasts only a "few days."

These factors, then, compounded the problem. The existence of good was questionable. There was only an earthly environment in which to seek it. And the time for seeking was short. No wonder that the Teacher plunged into the search with full vigor.

Like an eager boy at the county fair, pockets bulging with six months' allowance, he roamed from booth to booth tasting the goodies designed to heighten the senses. With wine he cheered his body while dulling his feelings of anguish or despair (2:3). With slaves, he eased his load of work, while increasing his sense of power (2:7). With wealth he enhanced his feelings of security, while indulging his every whim (2:8). With entertainers he whiled away his evenings, while satiating his drives in sexual pleasures (2:8).

All these experiences he drank to the bottom of the cup, and the pleasures he tasted heightened his senses—often to the point of ecstasy. But pleasure has another lure: it offers to *lift us above the routine*. So much of our living seems bound to the ordinary. It is hobbled by the patterns we learned in childhood; it is grooved by the habits we developed as teen-agers; it is fettered by the cords of conformity our culture puts upon us; it is kept on a narrow track by the duties of our daily jobs. Often we long to kick over the traces and bolt off on our own free course.

Pleasure lets us do that. Temporarily we can hang our inhibitions in the hallway and go to the party without them.

But not all pleasure is sheerly sensuous. The Preacher spoke of Solomon's pleasure in his accomplishments. Extraordinary achievements provide delight as they lift us above the routine:

> I made great works; I built houses and planted vineyards for myself; I made myself gardens and parks, and planted in them all kinds of fruit trees. I made myself pools from which to water the forest of growing trees. (Eccl. 2:4–6)

Useful, attractive, productive works these were, and satisfying. They began with a dream, took seed with a plan, started to bud as the building and planting began, and came to full flower in the grandeur of a palace and the verdure of a garden.

No one who has ever seen a dream come to fruition can doubt its pleasure—whether on the massive scale of Solomon's estates or in the simple matters of home-grown vegetables and hand-made furniture. To invent, to build, to garden, to paint—all these marvelously human acts can provide incredible pleasure.

The pleasures which heighten our senses and the pleasures which lift us above the routine play a mammoth role in our society. The thrill sought in drugs and drink, the relief from boredom craved in illicit sexual escapades, the preoccupation with gourmet foods and appropriate wines, the thirst for bizarre religious experience in the occult are just a few of the ways in which we seek to push back the frontiers of feeling and cross the boundaries into new sensations.

And what about the delight of high accomplishment? Few societies have driven themselves harder to achieve than ours. Who are the men and women we admire? The pace setters and the record breakers. Our list of heroes begins with persons who started with nothing and amassed great fortunes, who overcame hardship to rise to prominence, who shook off obscurity and rocketed to fame. Vicariously we savor their accomplishments to the last morsel. The pleasure of those who succeed helps to feed those who watch.

The Snare of Pleasure

Despite the high excitement and the quiet satisfaction which the pursuit of pleasure gave Solomon (Eccl. 2:10), the wise man branded the whole quest as futile. That is to say, the ultimate meaning in life, the highest good to which we should give ourselves, is not pleasure. The Preacher's last words on the subject were essentially the same as his first—except that they were even more doubtful about the values of what so many people live for:

> Then I considered all that my hands had done and the toil I had spent in doing it, and behold, all was vanity and a striving after wind, and there was nothing to be gained under the sun. (Eccl. 2:11)

" . . . My heart found pleasure in all my toil," the Preacher admitted, yet "all was vanity" (Eccl.

2:10–11). He knew the lure of pleasure, and he knew its snare. He had found that *pleasure promises more than it can produce*. Its advertising agency is better than its manufacturing department. It holds out the possibility of exquisite delight, but the best it can perform is titillation. It seeks to tickle the human spirit but cannot probe its depths. It daubs iodine on human wounds when what we need is surgery. It may distract us from our problems by diverting our attention, but it cannot free us from those problems.

It has another snare. *Pleasure satisfies only during the act*. Repetition is a key to pleasure. One drink, one sexual fling, one contest won, one project accomplished, one wild party—none of these, nor all of them put together, can be enough to bring satisfaction. The quest for pleasure is like eating salted peanuts; it is impossible to stop after the first bite. One bite leads to another because the first leaves no lasting impact. To reflect on the delights of the first peanut is far less gratifying than to reach for the second. And on it goes. Far from comforting us, each act of pleasure leaves us thirsty for the next.

One other snare needs mentioning. *The pursuit of pleasure results in either boredom or frustration*. Put simply, if we gain the pleasure we seek, we soon become tired of it. If we do not gain it, we are filled with disappointment. Those who give themselves to pleasure are often bored; those who wish they could and cannot are often bitter.

When pleasure's snares are examined we can see why the Preacher reached his negative conclusion. If you are looking for a foundation on which to build your life, do not count on pleasure. It does not have the permanence to sustain you. One or two days a year is all we can take even of something as beckoning as the county fair. What a hollow and futile life it would be to be locked within its gates permanently! The booths, contests and amusements that seem so enticing on rare occasions would cloy and nauseate us as a steady diet.

The Promise of Pleasure

It was a good warning that the Preacher gave us: even the richest, wisest, most accomplished of us will end up in futility if pleasure is our aim. To move beyond futility we must go another route.

It was Jesus—the greater than Solomon—who showed us the way. And it is a way that stands in sharp contrast to the Preacher's path of pleasure.

Pleasure there will be, Jesus promised, but it is not found by those who make seeking it their chief aim. True happiness will not come *apart from sharing Christ's suffering*. Who are the happy and blessed ones? Jesus' answer was plain: those who are poor in spirit, who mourn, who are hungry and thirsty for righteousness, who are persecuted for Christ's sake as they take up their cross and follow him.

And the true joy that Jesus promised will not be found *apart from serving Christ's purposes*. Not food, nor drink, nor raiment are our ultimate concern. "For the Gentiles seek all these things; and your heavenly Father knows that you need them all. But seek first his kingdom and his righteousness, and all these things shall be yours as well" (Matt. 6:32–33). To do God's work was why Christ came. There is no path beyond futility that does not merge with Christ's own way.

And most important, the true pleasure that Jesus promised will not be ours *apart from loving Christ's person.* When it comes down to it, what gives us fullest pleasure is not recreation, entertainment, accomplishment. It is fellowship. It is the intimate sharing of time, thoughts, experiences, and feelings with those for whom we care. Dutiful slaves and graceful dancing girls, charming gardens and lavish buildings, rich food and challenging games—all of these are no competition for the sheer delight of time spent with one we love.

Beyond futility—to pleasure? Only when we can give the right answer to the question that Jesus posed to Peter: " . . . do you love me more than these?" (John 21:15). To give the wrong answer is to be as foolish as a grown man who lingers over cotton candy at the county fair when his wife is waiting at home with the promise of intimate and satisfying love.

4 / Beyond Futility
  —to Permanence

Ecclesiastes 2:12–26

They were a wonder of the ancient world, and forty-five centuries after they were built we sons and daughters of a modern era still gaze at them in awe. The pyramids of Egypt, especially those at Giza, just outside of Cairo, are massive monuments to ancient technology. They demonstrate what can happen when a great civilization bends its back to achieve its purposes.

The Great Pyramid of the Pharaoh Khufu is staggering in size. Nearly 500 feet tall, it contains about 2,300,000 blocks of stone, each of which weighs at least two tons. Many comparisons have been used to try to convey an accurate impression of its vastness. One scholar has suggested that within its base there would be room for the great Italian cathedrals of Florence, Milan, and St. Peter's in the Vatican, as well as St. Paul's Cathedral and Westminster Abbey in London. One of the most striking comparisons comes from Napoleon's time. While some of his generals climbed to the top of the Great Pyramid, the Emperor waited below calculating the mass of stone in the three pyramids that jut up from the Giza plateau. When his generals descended Napoleon is said to have greeted them with this startling announcement: if all the stone in the three pyramids could be exported to France it would serve to build a wall ten feet high and one foot thick around the entire realm of France.

Why these massive pyramids? What purpose did they serve the Pharaohs who used thousands of workmen and decades of time in their building? Their aims were not just architectural. They had one chief goal in view as they emptied their coffers of gold, quarried their reserves of stone, preempted the skills of their engineers, and lashed at the backs of their laborers—they, the noble Pharaohs of the Old Kingdom, were *desperate to deal with death.*

Memorials the pyramids were, massive tributes to the memories of departed monarchs. As memorials they have served well. Still dominating the Nile to the east and the desert to the west, they remind all who see them of the awesome majesty of Egypt's bygone emperors. Memorials are one way of dealing with death. Large and lasting monuments confront later generations with the heroes of the past. We Americans have done just that with the beautiful stone tributes to the legacies of our presidents like Washington, Jefferson, Lincoln, and Kennedy.

But Egypt's Pharaohs had more in mind than memorials as they sought to deal with death. Here several things must be noted: first, the shape of the pyramid was probably patterned after the impression one gains in looking at the rays of the sun fan out from their single source as they shine on the earth; second, the Pharaohs of Egypt considered themselves as incarnations of the sun-god Ra; third, the ancient Egyptians believed that the dead had to be transported to the other world by some vehicle or conveyance (often a boat). When these points are put together, it seems reasonable to conclude that the chief purpose of the pyramid was to serve as a ladder, or better a staircase, to enable the departed king to make the steep ascent to his heavenly home. The pyramid, shaped like the falling rays of the sun, became the means by which the king returned to the sun, whence he had come to earth to rule among the men and women of Upper and Lower Egypt.

A desperate attempt to deal with death the pyramids were. Some kings spent most of their reign to prepare for its end.

Their giant tombs, then, are symbols of the transitory nature of our lives. Whatever we accomplish, whatever our station, however long we live— the end is the same, death. Its certainty is a constant reminder to commoner and king alike of our impermanence.

The Preacher who gave us his musings in the book of Ecclesiastes would have understood the pyramids and the kings who conceived them, because he too carried on all his labors in the shadow of death.

In fact, one of the compelling evidences in his argument about the futility of the things people depend on is the certainty of death. We use our wisdom and our resources to build sand castles that we deem attractive, and death like a giant bully stalks life's beaches and with a poke here and a kick there destroys the works of a lifetime.

The Ultimate Reality of Death

The Preacher continued to play the role of Solomon in testing the claims of the various candidates who were saying, "Vote for me, and I will show you life's meaning." *Wisdom's* credentials had been examined and found deficient, because wisdom cannot change reality; it can only seek to understand it; and, in understanding how bad reality can be, wisdom serves to increase our suffering. *Pleasure's* platform was also inadequate, despite the lavish campaign promises. Pleasure leads to frustration or boredom, because it only provides satisfaction during the moment that pleasure is being enjoyed and not beyond it. If we taste pleasure, we are soon bored; if we do not, we are often frustrated.

Next, then, the Preacher had Solomon explore the relationship of wisdom and folly to see whether one is really worth more than the other. Solomon assumed that his verdict would be accepted because no one who followed him would have greater opportunity or better resources to make such tests (Eccl. 2:12).

> Then I saw that wisdom excels folly as light excels darkness. The wise man has eyes in his head, but the fool walks in darkness; and yet I perceived that one fate comes to all of them. (Eccl. 2:13–14)

The ultimate reality of death makes wisdom's worth only relative. Given the choice of being wise or being foolish, one would choose wisdom as one would prefer bread to stone or cheese to chalk. Yet wisdom lacks permanent worth, because of death's relentless presence. Death is the "one fate" that catches both foolish and wise.

> Then I said to myself, "What befalls the fool will befall me also; why then have I been so very wise?" And I said to myself that this also is vanity. (Eccl. 2:15)

Vanity, our wise man called this—an empty shell, a trap of irony. All our lives we have been taught that wisdom pays, that prudence succeeds, that knowledge wins. And then comes death to undo all that we have learned. No final hope can be found in wisdom, because death outlasts it.

Beyond that, *the ultimate reality of death wipes out the memory even of the wise:*

> For of the wise man as of the fool there is no enduring remembrance, seeing that in the days to come all will have been long forgotten. How the wise man dies just like the fool! So I hated life, because what is done under the sun was grievous to me; for all is vanity and a striving after wind. (Eccl. 2:16–17)

We toil to build our little pyramids of remembrance, our modest monuments to our wisdom, and death sweeps over the terrain like a hot, dry sirocco and turns our pyramids into sand dunes—all of which look alike.

And death, the ultimate reality, has one other vicious whim: *it leaves all of our accomplishments for others to use:*

> I hated all my toil in which I had toiled under the sun, seeing that I must leave it to the man who will come after me; and who knows whether he will be a wise man or a fool? Yet he will be master of all for which I toiled and used my wisdom under the sun. This also is vanity. (Eccl. 2:18–19)

Futile and senseless it is, the Preacher complained, to pay the demanding price to acquire goods and wealth. We cannot take them with us—the wise man knew that. But what pained him even more was that an entirely unworthy heir might gain the comfort and glory.

No biblical passage paints a grimmer picture of what it costs to succeed on human terms and how fragile that success is. Listen to the harsh notes in this sad chant:

> What has a man from all the toil and strain with which he toils beneath the sun? For all his days are full of pain, and his work is a vexation, even in the night his mind does not rest. This also is vanity. (Eccl. 2:22–23)

Strain, toil, pain, vexation, insomnia—this is the currency with which we pay for success that we can neither truly gain nor keep.

We spend all our human resources and borrow against energy we do not have to build our pyramids by which to be remembered. Then death slips into the scene, erases our name from the cornerstone, and engraves in larger letters the name of someone less deserving. Our expensive legacy has been stripped from us by death, the consummate swindler.

The Reluctant Conclusion of Enjoyment

Death is a haunting reality diminishing the value of wisdom, erasing the memory of even the wise, and transferring our hard-earned gains to persons unsuited for them. All this the wise man made clear. Yet he did not counsel his pupils to give up on life. Instead, he came to a reluctant conclusion that modest enjoyment was possible. Three words of advice expressed this conclusion.

First, *enjoy life as you can:*

> There is nothing better for a man [or a woman] than that he should eat and drink, and find enjoyment in his toil. This also, I saw, is from the hand of God; for apart from him who can eat or who can have enjoyment? (Eccl. 2:24–25)

God, to Koheleth our Jewish Preacher, was not an absentee landlord. He was a gracious Provider, apart from whom we would not have either the basic provisions of life or its simple delights. The God of grace has given us freedom to enjoy his daily gifts. What we are not free to do is to presume on his grace or predict our own future, so we enjoy life as we can.

The second word of advice was this: *Surrender to God's decisions:*

> For to the man who pleases him God gives wisdom and knowledge and joy; but to the sinner he gives the work of gathering and heaping, only to give to one who pleases God. (Eccl. 2:26)

God it is who determines what kind of lot we have in life. And he does this on the basis of his evaluation of us. His decisions are final, though it is our duty to seek to please him. Since he alone knows what is best for us, we must surrender to his decisions and make the best of the lot he sends us.

This final word of counsel summed up the wise man's opinion: *Do not expect anything better.* We only brand life's results as vanity—as futility—if we hope for too much. It is false optimism that wounds us, according to the Teacher. If we try to guarantee our own permanence, if we try to build timeless pyramids through wealth, wisdom, pleasure, or achievement, we are doomed to futility. If we take God's gifts and decisions as they come and do not try to outwit God, we can snatch a measure of enjoyment from each day.

The Triumphant Solution of Resurrection

This reluctant conclusion has some merit to it. It keeps us from tacking our hopes to the crepe paper of tomorrow's wishes. It stirs us to seek joy in God's daily gifts. But it does little to help us face the ultimate reality of death. It has no power to assure us of the permanence we crave.

It took the greater Wise Man to do that. He replaced death as the ultimate reality when he said, "I am the resurrection and the life; he who believes in me, though he die, yet shall he live" (John 11:25). Resurrection is a triumphant solution to the problem of permanence. It takes us out of death's hands and places us under the power of a Savior who is himself the resurrection, the master of death.

As re-created persons, we will carry out a permanent mission—we will love and worship God through all eternity. Long after the biting sands and chipping winds have eroded the strong pyramids that guard the Nile, the resurrected people of God will live on to enjoy rich fellowship with their Maker and to praise the name of him who fully and finally has dealt with death.

5 / Beyond Futility
—to Freedom

Ecclesiastes 3:1–15

In some ways the red book is the most important piece of equipment in my office. About the size of a church hymnal, it sits in a prominent place on Inez' desk. Inez is my administrative assistant, and she is the keeper of that red book. If I press the buzzer twice, she will automatically pick up the book and bring it to my inner office, so that together we may consult it.

To some extent that book stands between us and utter confusion. It tells us which Tuesday to have lunch with a bishop, which Thursday to take the 8:45 AM flight to Chicago for a conference, which Monday the Seminary board will meet—and a thousand other things.

The red book on the desk contains our calendar for the year. In it all appointments are recorded—often months ahead of time. Once the schedules are set, that book comes close to being the governor of our lives. It sets the times by which we do things; it controls with almost rigid regularity our comings and goings.

And in so doing, it greatly limits our freedom.

We cannot face each day with the open question, what shall we do? We have to face it with the closed question, what have we already committed ourselves to do? Whatever regulates our time curtails our freedom.

That was the struggle the Preacher faced in one of the most famous passages in the book of Ecclesiastes. For him life was a red book in which all the key events were written by the hand of God with the result that men and women had no freedom either to alter them or understand them.

Futility, the Preacher called this lack of freedom. Futility—because our plans are limited, our ability to change our schedules is confined, our potential for affecting our own destiny is almost nil.

Contribute to Your Destiny

This grim conclusion put the Preacher at odds with many of the other wise men, particularly those whose sayings have been collected in the book of Proverbs. They were much more optimistic: "contribute to your destiny" was their motto. They advised their pupils to discover life's great principles and head in their direction.

By *hard work* they believed that they could make a contribution to their destiny:

A slack hand causes poverty,
   but the hand of the diligent makes rich.
A son who gathers in summer is prudent,
   but a son who sleeps in harvest brings shame.
      (Prov. 10:4–5)

The implication was clear: if we do the right thing at

the right time and do it well, we can shape our own prosperity.

Similarly, the wise teachers of Proverbs had taught their pupils that by *sound choices* they could contribute to their destinies:

> The wisdom of a prudent man is to discern his way,
> but the folly of fools is deceiving. (Prov. 14:8)

And again:

> Without counsel plans go wrong,
> but with many advisers they succeed. (Prov. 15:22)

Or this:

> Plans are established by counsel;
> by wise guidance wage war. (Prov. 20:18)

Diligence was one way to influence the future and discernment was another.

One of the qualities of a sound choice was to determine the right time for something to be said or done. In this way time could be used to advantage; its tides could be harnessed to carry their ship forward to its destiny:

> To make an apt answer is a joy to a man,
> and a word in season, how good it is! (Prov. 15:23)

Generations of young men and women were nurtured on this type of advice. They sought to know the right season for each type of work, and they believed that hard work and sound choices would pave their path to success. And then the Teacher in Ecclesiastes challenged everything they had been taught.

Submit to God's Determinations

The wise men in Proverbs had urged their students to humility. They should not take God's ways for granted:

> Many are the plans in the mind of a man,
>> but it is the purpose of the Lord that will be established. (Prov. 19:21)

But Koheleth (Ecclesiastes) argued that more than humility was needed. Total submission to what God had determined was the best that one could do.

God's planned time was the first evidence he offered in his argument.

> For everything there is a season, and a time for every matter under heaven:
> a time to be born, and a time to die;
> a time to plant, and a time to pluck up what is planted;
> a time to kill, and a time to heal;
> a time to break down, and a time to build up;
> a time to weep, and a time to laugh;
> a time to mourn, and a time to dance;
> a time to cast away stones, and a time to gather stones together;
> a time to embrace, and a time to refrain from embracing;
> a time to seek, and a time to lose;
> a time to keep, and a time to cast away;
> a time to rend, and a time to sew;
> a time to keep silence, and a time to speak;
> a time to love, and a time to hate;
> a time for war, and a time for peace. (Eccl. 3:1–8)

In line after line, the wise man reviewed life's most basic experiences and deepest emotions and concluded that each has its proper time. From the universal experience of birth and death to the practices of harvest, from the delights and restraints of marital love to the waging of war and the pursuit of peace—the Teacher reviewed the normal events in human life. His conclusion was bleak:

> What gain has the worker from his toil? (Eccl. 3:9)

The grey conclusion helps us understand Koheleth's point. The whole range of life—note that the events he lined out were all opposites—is beyond human control. Our toil is basically profitless because God has so planned and controlled the events in our life that all our efforts make almost no basic change.

Our frustrating restrictions were a major theme of the Preacher's argument. Submit to God's determinations, he has counseled, and accept his plans for your times. *His* plans are what count because our lives are restricted by the great gulf between him and us. The reason why our toil ends so profitlessly is stressed in these words:

> I have seen the business that God has given to the sons of men to be busy with. He has made everything beautiful in its time; also he has put eternity into man's mind, yet so that he cannot find out what God has done from the beginning to the end. (Eccl. 3:10–11)

Our ignorance of God's ways—this is the vexing problem. God controls our times, but he has not told us how and why. We walk in the dark, merely submitting to what God has determined, blind to his purposes, lame in our efforts to cooperate.

God's ways are good—"he has made everything beautiful in its time"—but he has kept us unaware of his ways or his timing. All of this is puzzling enough, but God has done something to tangle the puzzle further: "he has put eternity into man's mind." This is a difficult line to interpret. What it seems to mean is that God has placed within us a sense of concern for the future. We are made to be curious over our destiny, to wonder about our fate, to concern ourselves with where life is leading. Yet we can do so little about it. That was where the frustration sharpened for Ecclesiastes. Within humankind is the urge to know the future; God himself has placed that urge there. But we have no capacity to satisfy that urge. It is a sharp thirst beyond our power to quench. We yearn to be free enough to contribute to our destiny; we sense that there is a destiny that needs shaping; yet we do not have the freedom to do much about it, because God it is who determines the times of our life.

Where does all of this leave us? Our toil does not yield the profit we desire. Our struggle to understand the future is often fruitless. What can we do that is useful, enjoyable, meaningful, as we submit to God's determinations?

The Teacher answered these questions by pointing out *our limited possibilities*:

> I know that there is nothing better for them than to be happy and enjoy themselves as long as they live; also that it is God's gift to man that every one should eat and drink and take pleasure in all his toil. (Eccl. 3:12–13)

Full freedom we do not have, the Preacher concluded. God keeps the calendar of our lives. The red book that schedules our hours and days sits on his desk and is filled out by his hand. Our task is to submit to his determinations, but we are not to do this lying down. We do have possibilities for productive effort, for contributing to our welfare, for enjoying life. We should receive life as God's gift and make the best of it. The simple delights of food and drink and work come from his hand; they are tokens of his grace.

Grandiose plans we cannot make. Our attempts to have full freedom to form our own futures are futile. God sets our times and does so without letting us in on his secrets:

> I know that whatever God does endures for ever; nothing can be added to it, nor anything taken from it; God has made it so, in order that men should fear before him. (Eccl. 3:14)

Perhaps that verse says it best. God has fixed our courses and veiled them in mystery so that we may not take him for granted but may serve him in reverence and honor all our days.

Find Freedom Through Trust

This was not a bad conclusion that the Preacher had come to, but it was not a bright one either. He sailed under grey clouds, while we long for clear, blue skies. We may not want to have full control over our futures, but we would like to know more about them. We may be willing to leave tomorrow in God's hands, yet we would like to know better the God who programs our tomorrows.

Happily, Jesus Christ has come with just that information. He has put our problem of freedom into clear perspective. He has taught us to be humble about our knowledge of the future and yet to trust God's goodness as he leads us into it.

For Ecclesiastes, what hobbled and fettered true freedom was God's mysterious control. Jesus understood our human problem at a deeper level. What made our search for freedom futile was not God's determinism but our rebellion. Our human lust for freedom, acted out by Adam and Eve in the garden, brought a lifelong loss of freedom. Wanting freedom on our terms cost us true freedom on God's terms.

That was why Jesus had to do a new thing before true freedom became a reality: "So if the Son makes you free, you will be free indeed" (John 8:36). The new thing was that God's only Son had come. The rest of us are slaves, unable to free ourselves. Jesus came as the Son, the one who had ever and always been free. He—God's free one—had the power and the authority to share his freedom with us.

And what freedom it is! It is *the freedom to accept life as God gives it*. Ecclesiastes said almost the same thing, but he said it more grimly. Jesus knew the Giver better. He knew how grandly God can be trusted. And he urged us to find freedom through trust: "But if God so clothes the grass of the field . . . will he not much more clothe you, O men of little faith?" (Matt. 6:30). The God whom Jesus revealed can be fully trusted with the pages of our calendar. His love for us will not fail. Knowing that, we find freedom.

The darkest threats to our freedom he has defeated. The menace of judgment has been conquered by the power of forgiveness. The spectre of death has been put to flight by the wonder of resurrection. In Jesus Christ, God has shown himself to be a God of loving power and powerful love.

Far from feeling cramped by his control of our lives, we have the freedom to live today and to wait for tomorrow knowing that God's agenda is always what is best for us. The hand that writes the schedule in the red calendar book is a loving hand, in fact a hand that loved so much it endured nails for our sake.

Away with arrogance, then! We do not control our future, God does. And away with anxiety! The God who steers us into his future is a God whose trustworthiness has been thoroughly proven—by Jesus Christ and by all who have truly followed him.

6 / Beyond Futility —to Justice

Ecclesiastes 3:16–4:16

We want life's stories to have tidy endings. Though we enjoy happy endings, we do not insist upon them. We know that there are stories in life that do not end with the blissful couple strolling hand in hand toward the sunset. And we can accept stories with sad endings: Samson's final defeat of the Philistines costs him his own life; Romeo and Juliet die with their love unfulfilled; the king's horses and the king's men fail in their heroic efforts to reassemble Humpty Dumpty. Not all stories work out the way we would choose. But we learn to live with tinges of sadness.

What is harder to live with is injustice. We want our stories to have a tidy ending even if they do not end happily. We can cope with Cinderella's distress when the coach returns to a pumpkin at midnight. What we could not cope with would be the injustice of having the cruel step-sister rewarded rather than Cinderella. What would stun us would be to find out that the Lone Ranger was really a cattle-rustler or that Dick Tracy was a disguised chief of the Mafia.

Injustice is something that makes us all somewhat edgy if not downright uncomfortable. Fairness is a virtue we all intuitively prize. We want life's stories to have tidy endings—where all accounts are paid and all offenders punished. There is something wrenching and jarring to us to have the wicked turn out winners in the end. A world where that happened regularly would be more than we could bear.

It is probably a tribute to the influence of the Bible that we feel this way. So thoroughly have the prophets' concern for justice and Jesus' teaching about rewards permeated our thinking that we expect most of life's stories to end satisfactorily, even if they do not end happily. There may be an even deeper reason why we want this to happen: it may be a reflection of God's image within us. Though that image is tarnished by our sin, it has not been destroyed. It may cause our consciences to call to account those who offend our sense of justice, and it triggers reflexes within us when we experience or witness injustice.

Judicial sentiment, Edward John Carnell, my predecessor at Fuller Seminary, used to call this feeling. It is the sense of outrage that bubbles up within us when we feel that we or others close to us have been treated unfairly.

Judicial sentiment was something that the Preacher, whose observations on life are logged in the book of Ecclesiastes, felt keenly. He saw by his sharp and persistent investigations that some of life's stories—too many of them—ended untidily. His idea of justice, based as it was on the scriptural traditions of his people, was offended far too often. The verdict on life with which his book began—vanity of vanities, all is vanity—was confirmed by the lack of justice he observed in his society.

The Forms Injustice Takes

Like a many-headed monster, injustice threatened to destroy Koheleth's society and undermine all sense of right and wrong among its citizens. Oppression of the powerless, jealous competition among the aggressive, and compulsiveness on the part of the successful were three of the forms injustice took as it ravaged the countryside.

Oppression of the powerless often centered in the courts of law or the seats of government. It was this political oppression with which the Preacher began:

> Moreover I saw under the sun that in the place of justice, even there was wickedness, and in the place of righteousness, even there was wickedness. (Eccl. 3:16)

We can understand how disheartened the wise man must have been. We may tolerate a small gang of juvenile delinquents that vandalize a school or strip a car, as mean as those acts are. What we cannot tolerate is a judge of the juvenile court whose sentences are passed out by whim or whose favors are bought with a bribe. Where organized crime grows strong, we can take strong steps to quell it, but where the police force turns crooked, on what can the people depend?

Economic oppression seemed to have accompanied political injustice:

> Again I saw all the oppressions that are practiced under the sun. And behold, the tears of the oppressed, and they had no one to comfort them! On the side of their oppressors there was power, and there was no one to comfort them. (Eccl. 4:1)

The description was pitiful. From his wide-ranging knowledge and richly varied experience, the Preacher drew an irrefutable conclusion—oppression was rampant throughout our world ("under the sun") and the oppressed had few persons on their side to give them aid or comfort.

The age in which Ecclesiastes lived was far removed from the golden days of Israel's beginnings. The sense of concern for the poor, the widow, the alien, and the orphan had long since dimmed, outshone by the highly organized, commercial structures that had been borrowed from the Phoenicians and others. Apparently his was an age when the rich continued to acquire more, while the poor toiled ever harder to make ends meet. Wages were low, hours were long, rights were few. The oppressed had no way to express themselves except through tears, and no one to wipe those tears except other oppressed.

The Preacher's evaluation of the lot of these wretched souls, oppressed in the courts and in the markets, was bitter:

> And I thought the dead who are already dead more fortunate than the living who are still alive; but better than both is he who has not yet been, and has not seen the evil deeds that are done under the sun. (Eccl. 4:2–3)

What a drastic solution to the problem—to be dead or unborn was to be preferred to such oppression! What a cry of compassion from an otherwise stern observer—the sobs of the poor had fallen on sensitive ears!

Competition among the aggressive was another form injustice took:

> Then I saw that all toil and all skill in work come from a man's envy of his neighbor. (Eccl. 4:4)

The wise man had probed the subject of work before. He had concluded that hard work did not produce the results that teachers often promised their pupils. But here he dug deeper. He exposed the hollowness of much of our motivation for hard work—envy.

This was a painful observation. It undoubtedly unnerved his hearers as it unmasked their hypocrisy. They claimed to be toiling for all kinds of good motives—love for their family, concern for their community, service to their God. Rationalizations, the Preacher called these. At the bottom of the matter, the reason we work so hard is to keep up with or get ahead of our neighbors.

Think of the injustices to which envy may push us. We may be tempted to cheat our neighbors of their rights, to resent their accomplishments, to cut the corners of our own integrity—and all in the name of winning. The fabric of our communities gets torn into small pieces in our jealous competition. And the sense of concern for the welfare of others which is the heart of true justice becomes unraveled in the process. That was why the wise man branded so much of our toil as vanity, futility, emptiness.

When hard work caused such bitterness and strife, was it really to be as highly valued as some had taught? Ecclesiastes quoted a favorite proverb advocating hard work:

> The fool folds his hands, and eats his own flesh. (Eccl. 4:5).

Laziness is self-destructive, was the point. The Preacher's answer came in his own proverb, arguing for peace and harmony rather than for toil:

> Better is a handful of quietness than two hands full
> of toil and a striving after wind. (Eccl. 4:6)

Compulsiveness on the part of the successful was still
another form in which injustice showed itself:

> Again, I saw vanity under the sun: a person who has
> no one, either son or brother, yet there is no end to
> all his toil, and his eyes are never satisfied with
> riches, so that he never asks, "For whom am I toiling
> and depriving myself of pleasure?" This also is van-
> ity and an unhappy business. (Eccl. 4:7–8)

The drive to achieve and to acquire has awesome force. It nudges us from bed early and keeps us
in the factory or office late. Long after we have
enough to care for our own needs, some of us keep
pushing for more.

This compulsive drive can contribute to injustice, unless those who acquire wealth ask the question
that the Preacher posed, "For whom am I toiling and
depriving myself of pleasure?" The goods God has
given were not intended to make the rich richer. They
were intended to serve the needs of all God's people.
The drive to accumulate goods must be accompanied
by an urge to share them. If not, then injustice is the
sure result. Persons with ingenuity, energy, and opportunity can hoard huge resources while others go
begging.

The results are damaging both ways. Those
who have spend their health and peace in getting
more. Those who do not have become bitter and jealous toward those who have. For both, the result is a
futility that leaves life's story with an untidy ending.

The Remedies Life Provides

Wherever the wise man looked, injustice was at work. It crippled the legal system of the courts; it robbed the marketplace of its responsibility to enrich human life; it soured the motivation of the ambitious. Yet God was not absent, despite the inequities. The keen eye of the Preacher spotted remedies at work to keep injustice in check.

The power of fellowship was one of these remedies. The wise man described this power in words that have become justly famous:

> Two are better than one, because they have a good reward for their toil. For if they fall, one will lift up his fellow; but woe to him who is alone when he falls and has not another to lift him up. Again, if two lie together, they are warm; but how can one be warm alone? And though a man might prevail against one who is alone, two will withstand him. A threefold cord is not quickly broken. (Eccl. 4:9–12)

From the institution of marriage to the practice of collective bargaining, generations of people have tested the truth of these words. One of God's great gifts in helping us deal with problems of oppression, poverty, loneliness, and injustice is the company of others.

The lessons from experience are another remedy that life provides for the problems of injustice. Experience teaches us, according to Ecclesiastes, that those who abuse their power ultimately lose that power and pass into oblivion. As an illustration, the Preacher cited the case of a king who had begun his life in humble circumstances and then soared to power. Yet he seemed to forget his modest past and used his power selfishly and foolishly. In consequence his power was to fade and be forgotten despite the multitudes who called him king:

> There was no end of all the people; he was over all of them. Yet those who come later will not rejoice in him. Surely this also is vanity and a striving after wind. (Eccl. 4:16)

As Beethoven first admired Napoleon and then despised his cruel arrogance and his abuse of power, so experience teaches that life itself will exact punishment from those who hurt others with their wicked ambitions. But beyond that, *the fact of divine judgment* is the strongest remedy that life provides. Ecclesiastes saw that judgment as God's way of putting down human pride. Those whom God judges die like animals. Dust which has been our origin also becomes our destiny:

> God will judge the righteous and the wicked, for he has appointed a time for every matter, and for every work. I said in my heart with regard to the sons of men that God is testing them to show them that they are but beasts. For the fate of the sons of men and the fate of beasts is the same; as one dies, so dies the other. (Eccl. 3:17–19)

Let the unjust beware, and let us all be humble. The last words in life are God's. He has pledged himself to make the story come out fair—fair to all concerned including himself.

The Example Jesus Sets

This low, long cry for justice that Ecclesiastes voiced was picked up and sounded more strongly and more hopefully by Jesus. The example he set shows us best how to deal with life's injustices.

Where he could, he not only lamented over what was wrong in life, he did something about it. Think of the Temple money-changers cheating the worshipers in the very place where prayer to the living God was to be offered. Lashing them with whip and tongue, Jesus went after them and turned them out. Where he could not change the situation, as in his crucifixion, he bore with the injustice, while praying for those who persecuted him.

Both acts were deeds of love. His concern for human welfare, for human salvation, prompted him to firm intervention in one case and to strong intercession in the other.

What he did not do was to condone injustice or to despair over it. He acted in force and in love. He recognized its wrong and tried to help both those who were inflicting it and those who were afflicted by it.

He was acting as judge in both events. And he has a right to. He is the Father's appointed judge with whom all of us reckon now and will reckon in a day yet to come (Acts 17:31).

Futility was how the older wise man described a world fraught with injustice. He knew that the systems "under the sun" could not be depended on.

We know this, but we know more. We know that God is leading his people beyond futility to a concern for justice in every area of life. Beyond that we know personally the Lord who will judge all injustice and see to it that all life's stories have the tidy endings that we so earnestly yearn for.

7 / Beyond Futility
—to Worship

Ecclesiastes 5:1–7

Critics often rub us the wrong way, but we would find it hard to get along without them. Their opinions frequently seem harsh and arbitrary, and their judgments are rendered with a sarcasm that sometimes bites.

On television we watch them with eyes that squint questioningly. We shrug off their estimates of the state of music or art with a mild skepticism that says, "How do they know what is good or bad? How can they say what the rest of us should like?"

They rub us the wrong way, yet they render us a service. By describing an attractive art exhibit, they suggest how we can spend a profitable Saturday. When they pan a senseless play or a silly book they save us the effort and expense of finding out for ourselves. Who wants to waste an evening with a soprano that sings flat or a tenor that cracks on the high notes. Discerning critics often rescue us from such fates.

But they do more. When they do their work best, their discernment rubs off on us. We begin to sense the difference between great music and trite tunes, between contrived plots and compelling drama, between doggerel verse and well-crafted poetry, between the random splash of colors and distinguished art, between an entertaining adventure story and a life-molding novel. Where critics enhance our sense of beauty, invigorate our imagination or enlarge our appreciation of life, they have done us royal service. We are much the better for their work.

At times critics help us even more. I have in mind not only critics of the *arts* but also critics of our *society*. Theirs is the task of analyzing social trends and highlighting our social problems. They do this in many ways. Experts in consumer affairs point to some of the flaws in our advertising and merchandising practices. Social critics call attention to our moral trends. Marriage counselors analyze our changing attitudes toward the family and the impact they may have on the stability of our nation. Political journalists scrutinize the conduct of our government officials and expose their foibles. Humorists pinpoint our foolish attitudes.

All of these critics may rub us the wrong way at times, but we can scarcely do without them. They lay bare our prejudices, spotlight our weaknesses, and warn about our dangers. Overstatement, even exaggeration, is their loud way of getting our attention. But think what life would be without them. We would deceive ourselves and be bilked by others. Despite all their wild extravagance and pompous arrogance, critics make a valuable contribution to our society.

It was just this kind of contribution—the contribution of carping yet constructive criticism—that the Preacher, Ecclesiastes, tried to make. His society needed what he had to say. They had overvalued wisdom, almost to the point of using it to control God. They had overprized pleasure, hoping by it to find life's true meaning. They had perverted justice by diminishing the rights of the poor and the oppressed. And they had overestimated their freedom to make life-shaking decisions, by ignoring the mystery of God's ways. A futile way of life was what the Preacher accused them of living. With his sharp pen he had pricked the balloons of their hollow hopes.

A Religion Gone Stale

Their religious practices did not escape his keen eye. Usually the wise men left such matters as prayer, sacrifice, vows, and rituals to the priests who were in charge of the Temple. But not Ecclesiastes. Fake religion distressed him as much as proud wisdom, vain pleasure, abused justice, or hollow freedom.

Apparently the people took a mechanical attitude toward the sacrifices which God had commanded. They were offering them in huge volume and with great attention to detail. But they were missing the deeper meaning, the key purpose, of those animal offerings. *Listening to God is better than sacrifice* was the Preacher's word to them:

> Guard your steps when you go to the house of God; to draw near to listen is better than to offer the sacrifice of fools, for they do not know that they are doing evil. (Eccl. 5:1)

"The sacrifice of fools" was empty sacrifice, going through the ritual but missing its meaning. What was the basic purpose of the offerings that God required? It was communion with God. Therefore, they dealt with the major human needs: they brought forgiveness, when accompanied by a contrite heart; they expressed thanksgiving, when the offerer was truly grateful; they fulfilled vows, when God had brought unusual blessing. The sacrifices were the means by which God's people were to declare their total dependence on him. Listening—paying attention to God—then, was an essential requirement, if the sacrifices were to have any meaning.

What were the Preacher's countrymen doing wrong? They were treating sacrifices like magic. They thought blood and smoke were what God wanted. They forgot that spirit and heart were essential ingredients of true sacrifice. The words of the psalm had escaped their minds:

> For thou hast no delight in sacrifice;
>> were I to give [only] a burnt offering, thou
>> wouldst not be pleased.
> The sacrifice acceptable to God is a broken spirit;
>> a broken and contrite heart, O God, thou wilt
>> not despise. (Ps. 51:16–17)

What Samuel had told Saul, they needed once again to hear:

> "Behold, to obey is better than sacrifice,
>> and to hearken than the fat of rams." (1 Sam.
>> 15:22)

A religion gone stale needed sharp criticism, and Ecclesiastes did not hesitate to give it.

The wise man's second criticism followed closely his first. Not only is listening to God better than sacrifice, but *brevity in prayer is better than extravagance:*

> Be not rash with your mouth, nor let your heart be
> hasty to utter a word before God, for God is in
> heaven, and you upon earth; therefore let your
> words be few. (Eccl. 5:2)

Again, the Preacher wanted to remind his hearers of
the greatness of God who could see through any extravagance in prayer. Wild promises, unguarded
commitments, vain repetition were all to be avoided.

Prayer was solemn conversation with a mysterious God. The vast gap between humankind and
him demanded sobriety, not extravagance. Neither
the volume, nor the eloquence, nor the frequency of
prayers were what influenced him. In no way could
he be manipulated into answering prayer. What he
would hear were the simple, sincere, brief words of
those who truly submitted to his majesty and sought
his help. Any other approach was as full of fantasy as
a wild dream. The Preacher illustrated his point with
a proverb:

> For a dream comes with much business, and a fool's
> voice with many words. (Eccl. 5:3)

A religion gone stale permitted vain, dream-like
babbling as a substitute for prayer. No wonder the
Preacher took pains to point out its futility.

The Preacher's last criticism dealt with the
vows that people rashly offered. This was his word:
faithfulness in keeping vows is better than fickleness. Here
is how he put it:

> When you vow a vow to God, do not delay paying
> it; for he has no pleasure in fools. Pay what you
> vow. It is better that you should not vow than that
> you should vow and not pay. (Eccl. 5:4–5)

69

Vows played a prominent part in the lives of Israel's men and women. A vow was one way to show how seriously they took their need of God. In times of emergency they used vows to underline their prayer requests. A barren woman who longed for a son, a frightened soldier under enemy attack, an innocent person accused of serious crime each might vow to offer a special sacrifice to God if he would deliver him or her from the predicament.

How easy it was to vow, and how hard to pay! That was the tendency Ecclesiastes criticized. Apparently one way to get out of the vow was to tell the priest (called here "the messenger") that it was a mistake. In stern words that threatened God's judgment, Ecclesiastes warned against this:

> Let not your mouth lead you into sin, and do not say before the messenger that it was a mistake; why should God be angry at your voice, and destroy the work of your hands? (Eccl. 5:6)

Then, good wise man that he was, Ecclesiastes clinched his point with a proverb:

> For when dreams increase, empty words grow many: but do you fear God. (Eccl. 5:7)

Babbling, rambling, wild words may be alright in dreams, but they do not belong in worship. Our relationship to God is one of sober, respectful, reverent awe—"but do you fear God"—not of hasty vows which have to be retracted by cheating.

By now we have gotten the Preacher's message. He has been saying that God must be taken with unconditional seriousness. He was saying, further, that his countrymen had failed to do that. Yet like

most critics he was better at exposing the weaknesses
of his people than he was at helping them be strong.
Many critics can tell when a singer like Beverly Sills
has an off night; none of them can sing better than she
does on any night. Social analysts can chart the drift
of our society much more readily than they can steer
us on a safer course.

A Worship Made Vital

Where religion has gone sour, where religious exercise
has replaced true worship, more than criticism is
needed. One of Jesus' most powerful words spoke to
this need:

> "But the hour is coming, and now is, when the true
> worshipers will worship the Father in spirit and
> truth, for such the Father seeks to worship him.
> God is spirit, and those who worship him must wor-
> ship in spirit and in truth." (John 4:23–24)

Here Jesus came to the heart of the matter.
The reason that we must take our worship seriously is
that God's own nature demands it. As spirit, that is as
ultimate and infinite Person, our heavenly Father
longs for communion with his people, not for hollow
symbols or empty actions. False worship is as much
an affront to him as obscene insults are to a wife or
husband. Better to bribe a judge than to ply God with
hollow words; better to slap a policeman than to seek
God's influence by meaningless gestures; better to
perjure yourself in court than to harry God with
promises you cannot keep. The full adorations of our
spirit, the true obedience of our heart—these are his
demands and his delights.

In spelling out what this means, Jesus took us much further than Ecclesiastes ever could. *Beyond listening to deeds of mercy* was where Jesus wanted to take us. His rebuke of the Pharisees who opposed him was sharp: "Go and learn what this means. 'I desire mercy, and not sacrifice.' For I came not to call the righteous, but sinners" (Matt. 9:13). Like the men of Ecclesiastes' day, some of the Pharisees were relying on the merits of their sacrifices to please God; they were not listening to him as the Preacher had suggested. Had they listened, they would have heard God's call for them to show mercy to others—others like the crooked tax-collectors and law-breakers to whom Jesus brought good news. The worship made vital that Jesus offered as a replacement of the religion gone stale had to result in mercy and kindness to others. God's very nature as a merciful God insisted on it.

Lessons in prayer were also part of Jesus' curriculum. *Beyond brevity to full trust in a loving Father* was where he wanted to lead us:

> "And when you pray, you must not be like the hypocrites; for they love to stand and pray . . . at the street corners, that they may be seen by men. . . . And in praying do not heap up empty phrases as the Gentiles do; for they think that they will be heard for their many words . . . for your Father knows what you need. . . . Pray then like this: Our Father who art in heaven. . . ." (Matt. 6:5, 7–9)

The contrast is obvious. The Preacher urged brevity in prayer because of God's majesty ("for God is in heaven, and you upon earth"); Jesus advised brevity because of God's compassion. A loving Father can be trusted to know and meet our needs. Not stale religion but vital worship of this Father was what Jesus made possible.

Jesus also taught about the keeping of vows. As he did, he guided his followers *beyond faithfulness to transparency of heart:* "... it was said to the men of old, '... perform to the Lord what you have sworn.' But I say ... Let what you say be simply 'Yes' or 'No' " (Matt. 5:33–34,37). Not elaborate oaths, even faithfully kept, are Jesus' new way; but simple affirmations of what we will do or not do. Obedience so steady that it needs no oath to prop it up—that is a fruit of vital worship.

Two words we have heard. Our society needs to hear them both. The word of warning from the critic and the word of rescue from the Savior. We need firm warning where church attendance and church activity have substituted for listening to God's voice, where prayer has become a selfish exercise in begging, where promises made to God in stress are forgotten in leisure.

But we need more than firm warning. We need strong rescue. He who comes from the Father and shows us what the Father is like has provided it. He has pointed the way to vital worship. More than that, he himself has *become* the Way.

8 / Beyond Futility
   —to Wealth

Ecclesiastes 5:10–6:8

I kept wondering as I watched the gold ball bounce from bumper to bumper. It was just a game on television but it set me wondering about a basic question in life. The bouncing of the gold ball was worth money to the contestant—$200 per bounce. I wondered as the audience screamed in sheer delight; I wondered as the player jumped and shrieked for joy.

My question was simple: why do we find the hope of acquiring wealth so exciting? That bouncing ball was not really going to change the life of the person participating in the game. It could not heal any disease, solve any marital problems, or guarantee him security on his job. Yet his excitement suggested it could do all three. And so did the excitement of the studio audience who cheered and sighed as the ball rolled from success to danger. This scene at the studio was being eyed by an audience of millions at home who daily share the emotional thrill of this or other game shows where instant wealth is the aim. Instant wealth—think of the lure it has held for human minds and hands. For it pirates attacked ships bearing precious cargo; for it prospectors slogged mountain trails behind their burros; for it conquistadors sailed the Spanish Main and massacred a host of Indians; for it gamblers flood the casinos of Las Vegas; for it a multitude of people play the monthly lotteries and enter the magazine sweepstakes.

Why? Why the lust for wealth, the almost *universal* lust for wealth? Probably because wealth is viewed as power. Some see it as the power to create more wealth. How often we greet the news of a successful investment with the response, "It takes money to make money." For others wealth means the power to get your own way. A woman in the Los Angeles ghetto was explaining why there was a violent shootout in her neighborhood where six people were killed, while no blood was shed when Patty Hearst was captured in San Francisco. Her explanation was simple: "The rich can always get things done their way."

My point is not to justify these feelings about wealth, but only to try to understand why wealth has such attraction to those who do not have it. In the world of the Bible, many viewed wealth not only as power to create more wealth or as power to get things done the way one wanted, but as a sign of God's blessing. After all, many of the prominent figures of biblical history were allowed to garner huge wealth: Abraham, Jacob, Joseph, David, Solomon, to name a few. And some proverbs taught that righteousness would lead to wealth:

> In the house of the righteous there is much treasure,
>   but trouble befalls the income of the wicked.
>   (Prov. 15:6)

And again:

75

> A good man leaves an inheritance to his children's
>   children,
> but the sinner's wealth is laid up for the righteous.
>   (Prov. 13:22)

Undoubtedly words like these made the people yearn for the wealth that was a sign of blessing, rather than for the righteousness that might, in God's time, lead to prosperity. It was this almost compulsive concern with material possessions that led to some of Ecclesiastes' strongest words.

The Frustration of Seeking Material Goods

> He who loves money will not be satisfied with money; nor he who loves wealth, with gain: this also is vanity. (Eccl. 5:10)

This was the first in a series of arguments which the Preacher used to show the frustration that comes to persons who seek material goods as a prime ambition in life. *Wealth cannot satisfy* was the point with which Ecclesiastes began.

There is something about the drive to acquire that impels us to seek more and more. Few people have the discipline to say "Enough; I need no more." If it is insecurity that prods us to seek wealth, wealth itself will not cure that insecurity. If it is the desire for power that pushes us, money will not quell that desire. For many people the thirst for more material goods is insatiable. Long after their basic needs are met, they crave for more. Long after they have the permanent security they seek, they strive for more. Long after they have all the luxuries they covet, they itch for more.

Vain, futile—that kind of life. All enjoyment

of what these people do have is clouded by the thought of what they want next. All gratitude for present blessing is overshadowed by the fear of tomorrow's losses. All generosity may shrivel because the wealthy person is preoccupied not with how he can help others, but with what he can gain next.

"You'll never get anything from him," a friend of mine declared flatly. We had been discussing a prospective donor to Fuller Seminary. "Your only chance is to get something from his widow." I was puzzled by my friend's bluntness. "Money means power to that man," he went on to explain. "All his life he has been acquiring goods and land. Acquisition is his way of life. It is psychologically impossible for him to give any substantial amount away." Sad to say, my friend was right. That industrious and frugal man fit Ecclesiastes' words to a tee: he loved money yet never had enough to be satisfied with it.

> When goods increase, they increase who eat them; and what gain has their owner but to see them with his eyes? (Eccl. 5:11)

This was the Preacher's second bit of evidence in his argument that seeking material goods was a frustrating way of life. *Wealth attracts idle hangers-on.* Would-be friends and long-lost relatives appear as from nowhere when the word of wealth spreads. Even though the Preacher lived in a highly organized and complexly commercial society, the old customs of kinship and hospitality had not disappeared. Friends and relations could still lay some claim on the wealth of their loved ones. And these claims often proved burdensome to the wealthy.

The wise men in Proverbs had viewed the friendly attention that wealth brings more positively:

Many seek the favor of a generous man,
> and every one is a friend to a man who gives gifts.
All a poor man's brothers hate him;
> how much more do his friends go far from him.
> (Prov. 19:6–7)

A mixed blessing at best, Koheleth, the Preacher, called this. Friends and family gather around wealth. They may pester the rich person and dissipate what he has. How often have we read of an athlete—say, a boxer—whose golden moments found him surrounded by an entourage that gladly shared his wealth, but whose twilight days saw him both broke and abandoned. Wealth can carry its own frustration—that was the Preacher's apt observation.

> Sweet is the sleep of a laborer, whether he eats little or much; but the surfeit of the rich will not let him sleep. (Eccl. 5:12)

The argument proceeded. Wealth not only fails to satisfy and attracts fair-weather friends, but also *wealth increases anxiety*. Here the Preacher's point was not so much the anxiety over the responsibilities of wealth, as it was the anxiety caused by the use of wealth. Fancy parties, rich food, high living—none of these is conducive to relaxation. The overindulgence which wealth makes possible and the stress which fame and attention produce all work against sleep. And where sleep flees, hardly anything else in life can truly be enjoyed. Insomnia is much more likely to occur in the fancy houses on the hilltops than in the small cottages in the valley. Wealth may bring frustration in many forms. And sleeplessness is surely one of the more vexing.

Wealth is easily lost. That was the Preacher's

next argument, and one that he labored at length. He based it on his personal observations of the way life works.

> There is a grievous evil which I have seen under the sun: riches were kept by their owner to his hurt, and those riches were lost in a bad venture; and he is father of a son, but he has nothing in his hand. (Eccl. 5:13–14)

Each of us can add his own illustrations to this. Gain with money is usually related to risk. Fortunes have been made in oil. Huge companies have been founded, and numbers of families—from the Rockefellers to the Hunts—have acquired affluence through investments in oil. But think of the dry holes! Probably four of them have been drilled for each well that has brought in oil. As much money has been lost in oil exploration as has been earned—perhaps more.

Rarely will there be great return on investment without great risk. Stock market, commodity exchange and real estate investment all demonstrate this. Wealth drives us to acquire more wealth. That was the Preacher's first argument. Then pointedly he coupled that with his story about the dangers of loss. We are pushed to make more, he has told us, yet that very push puts us in jeopardy of losing everything and of leaving our family as paupers.

> This also is a grievous evil: just as he came [i.e. naked], so shall he go; and what gain has he that he toiled for the wind. . .? (Eccl. 5:16)

A frustrating affair it can be to build your life on the getting of wealth.

The Preacher capped his case with one more line of evidence, again based on personal observation:

> There is an evil which I have seen under the sun,
> and it lies heavy upon men: a man to whom God
> gives wealth, possessions, and honor, so that he
> lacks nothing of all that he desires, yet God does not
> give him power to enjoy them, but a stranger enjoys
> them; this is vanity; it is a sore affliction. (Eccl.
> 6:1–2)

Whether it was death or fraudulence that cheated a person of his wealth the Preacher did not say. Both may block full enjoyment of what one has.

A person develops a new product and then calls in someone else to help him market it. Before long, the newcomer has taken over and the inventor has been robbed of his rights. A person toils for years to build a business and is snatched by death at the moment the business turns a comfortable profit. These are the vexations the Preacher had in mind. Solemn reminders they are of the frustrations that one faces if getting rich is his chief aim, including the frustration that *wealth can readily be taken from us.* We should remember that as we watch the ball bounce its way through the marble machines. Neither instant wealth nor long-term wealth can accomplish all they promise. Their failure to do that sharpens our frustration.

The Satisfaction of Seeking Spiritual Wealth

The best answer that the Preacher could give to these frustrations was that we should enjoy our wealth, not try to hoard it:

> Behold, what I have seen to be good and to be fitting
> is to eat and drink and find enjoyment in all the toil

with which one toils under the sun the few days of
his life which God has given him, for this is his lot.
(Eccl. 5:18)

This is not bad advice. It reminds us that what we
have is a gift of God, created and provided by him.
Like all of his creation, these gifts are good. They are
not to be despised or rejected, but to be enjoyed.

But more needed to be said. And as usual we
can count on Jesus, the wise man greater even than
Solomon, to say the needful things. *Contentment is
more satisfying than wealth* was one of Jesus' words.
The truth of this word he demonstrated in his own
life. Without a place to lay his head, he lived content-
edly knowing that his loving Father would supply all
his need. Whether treated shabbily by Jewish leaders
or entertained lavishly by wealthy admirers, he was
ready to make the most of his circumstances by prac-
ticing what he preached: "Therefore do not be anxious, saying, 'What shall we eat?' or 'What shall we
drink?' or 'What shall we wear?'... Your heavenly
Father knows that you need them all" (Matt. 6:31–32).

*Doing God's will is more important than gaining
goods.* That was another word that Jesus gave to take
us beyond the futility and frustration of the quest for
wealth. His story of the man who acquired vast lands
and built huge barns is painfully clear. God sabotaged
his plans and rebuked him for them: " 'Fool! This
night your soul is required of you; and the things you
have prepared, whose will they be?' So is he who lays
up treasure for himself, and is not rich toward God"
(Luke 12:20–21).

"Rich toward God"—what an apt description
of the direction God wants us to head. We do not
jump up and down in front of life's marble machines,

greedy for instant gain. We gratefully receive what we have and then put it to God's purposes: our modest enjoyment and his faithful service.

And when we do this, Christ's third word becomes true for us: *Doing God's will brings the highest wealth of all.* On one occasion, Peter and the other disciples wondered whether their sacrifice of leaving jobs and homes to go with Jesus would be recognized.

> Jesus said, "Truly, I say to you, there is no one who has left house or brothers or sisters or mother or father or children or lands, for my sake and for the gospel, who will not receive a hundredfold now in this time, houses and brothers and sisters and mothers and children and lands, with persecutions, and in the age to come eternal life." (Mark 10:29–30)

Talk about investments—one hundredfold Jesus promised, and at no risk except persecution. For God himself is the Guarantor of the returns. And talk about wealth! Life's marble machines that promise instant gain are exposed as tawdry toys in the face of the profit Jesus promised—eternal life. It is his grace—not our gain—that leads us beyond the frustrations of earthly wealth to the riches that bring full satisfaction: the riches of fellowship with God now and forever.

9 / Beyond Futility —to Hope

Ecclesiastes 6:9–7:29

They may be the grimmest words we ever hear. The surgeon comes through the swinging doors of the waiting room, his green gown patched with sweaty stains. His steps are halting, his eyes are clouded, his words are faltering: "No hope."

Or the pediatrician hovers over the incubator, his stethoscope glued to a tiny chest. The parents press their faces to the window of the cubicle in sheer dismay, as the physician slowly straightens up, drapes the stethoscope around his neck, and shakes his head with fearful finality: "No hope."

The words bombard the ears and addle the brain. They are heard daily in a hundred hospitals, but we never get used to them. Life without hope carries more trauma than the human spirit can bear.

That was one reason why the message of Ecclesiastes, the Old Testament Preacher, hit his hearers with such shock. Like a master internist he fingered humanity's wrist, listened to the chest, checked the whites of the eyes, reviewed the medical chart, and uttered the solemn pronouncement: "No hope."

Look at Life and Abandon Hope

As he often did, the Professor began his argument with his conclusion, this time in the form of a proverb:

> Better is the sight of the eyes than the wandering of desire; this also is vanity and a striving after wind. (Eccl. 6:9)

The closest English equivalent to this proverb is probably, "A bird in the hand is worth two in the bush." Be content with what you have—your work, your food, your family—do not hope for what is beyond your reach. What you see with your eyes you can count on; what you crave with your soul you probably will not attain.

The Preacher would surely apply this verse to all the treasures that his friends were vainly striving after. Do not spend yourself, he has warned, reaching for meaning, for wisdom, for pleasure, for freedom, for permanence, for justice, for wealth that are beyond your grasp. He would also apply this text to the subject of hope. He might support the observation that hope springs eternal within the human breast, but he would quickly add that such hope is vanity. Life will not get better. Any hope we hold to is grounded in fantasy, unreality, false perception. Look at life, he counseled, and abandon hope.

The future is too mysterious to encourage hope. Thus he began his argument:

> For who knows what is good for man while he lives the few days of his vain life, which he passes like a shadow? For who can tell man what will be after him under the sun? (Eccl. 6:12)

A mysterious future means an uncertain present. If we do not know our ultimate destiny, how can we tell if we are on the right road? When we cannot say how life will turn out tomorrow, how can we decide what is good for us to do today?

"No hope," the Preacher shook his head. Waste no time dreaming of rosy futures. Just enjoy life as it comes right now. What you do not know will not hurt you, unless you plan on its being better than it really is. If you do, disappointment is inevitable.

A mysterious future dampens hope, but even more chilling is the certainty of death. *Death is too certain to allow for hope.* Here the Preacher returned to a familiar theme—the reality of death which darkens all human optimism, which scrambles all human plans, which shatters all human dreams. Ecclesiastes chose a startling strategy of presentation in describing death. Death is the great reality, so it is to be preferred even to birth, which does little for us but launch us on the seas of suffering. With a chain of proverbs the wise man tied together his thoughts on death, the great enemy of hope:

> A good name is better than precious ointment;
> and the day of death, than the day of birth.
> It is better to go to the house of mourning
> than to go to the house of feasting;
> for this is the end of all men,
> and the living will lay it to heart.
> Sorrow is better than laughter,
> for by sadness of countenance the heart is made glad.
> The heart of the wise is in the house of mourning;
> but the heart of fools is in the house of mirth.
> (Eccl. 7:1-4)

Strong words, dark words! But the Preacher would have called them realistic. He had looked at the certainty of death, and it loomed so large that it dwarfed life. Death, not life, was the dominant issue to be faced. In the light of it, mirth and laughter were a luxury only fools could indulge in. The wise and the serious had to pay their full attention to death.

To sing a song of hope, to whistle a tune of expectation, to let loose a laugh of anticipation in such darkness was the height of folly. His opponents may have chided him with words like, "Come now, Koheleth, relax, cheer up, life is not so grim as your picture of it." But the Preacher would have none of it. Such optimism, such hope, was fearfully misleading in his view. And he bluntly told his opponents so:

> It is better for a man to hear the rebuke of the wise
>   than to hear the song of fools.
> For as the crackling of thorns under a pot,
>   so is the laughter of the fools;
>   this also is vanity. (Eccl. 7:5–6)

No hope, the Preacher gloomily pronounced. Because death is the end of us all, it should claim our attention and spare us the bitter disillusionment of a hope that cannot be.

Something else the wise man wrote shows us why he held that all hope was futile. *Humankind is too sinful to have reason for hope.* In his role as a shrewd observer of life, the Preacher claimed to have made ample study of human nature. His conclusion was grey, especially his judgment on treacherous women:

> And I found more bitter than death the woman whose heart is snares and nets, and whose hands are fetters; he who pleases God escapes her, but the sinner is taken by her. (Eccl. 7:26)

Such treachery is the norm, not the exception, among

both men and women, according to the Preacher's research:

> One man among a thousand I found, but a woman among all these I have not found. (Eccl. 7:28)

Meanness, crookedness, arrogance, and deceit are most visible human attributes—found almost universally. In the Preacher's experience one man in a thousand and no woman could be fully counted on to do what is right. Men can take no comfort from this passage—any supposed superiority here is trivial, one tenth of one percent to be exact. And had someone besides our skeptical wise man been doing the counting, the odds might have even favored the women!

The point is that there is every reason, given our distorted human nature, not to hold out hope. When the Preacher added up the sum of his investigations, he tells us,

> Behold, this alone I found, that God made man upright, but they have sought out many devices. (Eccl. 7:29)

Will a just God bless the rosy dreams or confirm the wishful thinking of a human family that has so perverted his purposes?

"No hope!" Like a tightlipped surgeon still stunned by the sounds and smells of death, the Preacher mouthed his desperate verdict: Look at life—with its mysterious future, with its certain death, with its wicked ways—look at life, and abandon hope.

The same realism that made the Teacher suspect all hope made him stress practical wisdom as a way of struggling through life. As at other points he had urged his hearers to settle for simple delights like work, food, drink, fellowship, so here he counseled them to resist the temptations of bribery (7:7); to exercise patience, not pride (7:8); to control their anger (7:9); to abstain from a nostalgia for the good old days (7:10); to submit to the will of God which man does not have power to change (7:13); to avoid a compulsive commitment either to righteousness or wickedness (7:16–17); to fear God (7:18); and to ignore malicious comments that others may make about them (7:21–22).

In a world where one faced futility on every hand, this was probably sane advice. At least it was the best the Teacher—given his view of life and his time in history—could do. He had lost touch with the great promises of the earlier wise men who had offered hope to the people in words like these:

> The hope of the righteous ends in gladness,
>   but the expectation of the wicked comes to
>   nought. (Prov. 10:28)

To Ecclesiastes' eyes, that clear distinction between the righteous and the wicked had become blurred and his whole view of hope was clouded as a result. More than that, he was tone-deaf to the songs of the prophets that rang with hope about the latter days when God's glory and righteousness would be revealed to Israel and the world.

No hope, just some sage counsel was the best he could do. But all of us need more than that.

Trust Christ and Find Hope

One reason why Jesus' message blew through the ancient world like a gust of fresh air was that it carried new hope, great hope. It shed brilliant light on a future that for Koheleth and his students was shrouded with gloom.

With considerable wisdom and with abundant candor, Ecclesiastes had shown the weaknesses in human views of hope. He had taught his followers in what not to hope; but it took Jesus to show the human family where full hope could be found. The Preacher's motto was "Look at life and abandon hope." Jesus' word was better: "Trust me and find hope."

Ecclesiastes' conclusion was buttressed by three lines of argument. Jesus answered each of them. That the future is too mysterious to encourage hope was the Preacher's opinion. Jesus' answer was *the hope of a glorious coming*, bright with power and righteousness. Many times he described it in phrases like these:

> "and they will see the Son of man coming on the clouds of heaven with power and great glory; and he will send out his angels with a loud trumpet call, and they will gather his elect from the four winds, from one end of heaven to the other." (Matt. 24:30–31)

What a climax to history! What a destiny for God's people! Not only spectators but full participants in the fulfillment of God's great plan to make his name known across the earth! Who can cry "No hope" in the light of that stupendous event?

That death is too certain to allow for hope was Koheleth's judgment. Jesus' answer was *the promise of resurrection and eternal life:*

> "for the hour is coming when all who are in the tombs will hear his voice and come forth, those who have done good, to the resurrection of life, and those

who have done evil, to the resurrection of judgment." (John 5:28–29)

Death's lease on human life has been broken; since Christ's resurrection the human family has been under new ownership. Resurrection is the destination of us all. But only those who truly trust Jesus as God's full truth can really hope in resurrection.

For them death is no longer a nemesis which tramples plans and mocks achievements. It is a portal of hope—death is—leading to resurrection and eternal friendship with God. Who can whisper "No hope" in the face of that resurrection?

That humankind is too sinful to have reason for hope was Ecclesiastes' conclusion. Jesus' shattered it with *the offer of full forgiveness*. It was to those who recognize their sinfulness that Jesus came. They are the lost sheep which the Shepherd carries home from the wilderness; they are the lost coins that the woman joyfully finds; they are the prodigal sons whom the Father enthusiastically welcomes (Luke 15). Who can mutter "No hope" in the sight of that welcome?

When the physicians of this world's problems have exhausted their skill in social reform, economic theory, educational philosophy, and political strategy, they will shake their heads and sigh "No hope." But theirs is not the last word. Jesus came to do God's full work—the full work of the God of Hope (Rom. 15: 13).

10 / Beyond Futility
—to Authority

Ecclesiastes 8:1–9:18

Our attitude toward authority tends to be ambivalent. We are like the eighteen-year-old lad who joins the army to find security and learn discipline and then resents that first military haircut. He wants to have his life organized, but not to the point of polishing his buttons and shining his shoes. He longs to know who he is and how he fits into life, but he would rather find this out by other ways than close order drill or double time marches.

Ambivalence toward authority—I suppose we learn it in our families almost from birth. We want the security of parents who support us and guide us as we grow, yet we chafe under their correction and squirm to escape their regulations.

Certainly part of the problem is ours. Human sin, in the first place, was a contest of authority. What God had ordered, our first parents had rejected. They pitted their will against his word and set a pattern of rebellion that all of their descendants—with one exception—have followed.

But part of the problem with authority is that

those who wield it are also rebels. Drill sergeants and parents, school teachers and bosses, playground directors and kings are all in revolt against authority—in some measure, at least.

So the ambivalence is fed from both sides. Those who exercise authority are prevented from doing it well by their own conflicts with it, and those whose lot is to follow drag their feet because they resent being pushed around by others. Yet both groups know that without authority little in life can be accomplished. When leaders will not lead or followers will not follow, something akin to chaos is the result.

Probably nobody in the Old Testament sensed the ambivalence that we feel toward authority more acutely than Ecclesiastes, the wise Preacher. With sharp insight, he had observed the ways of kings and commoners and the conflict between them caused by the use and abuse of authority. The problem of authority he saw as part of the futility with which life is marked. Just as wisdom, pleasure, and wealth offer much less than they appear to, so authority as a good goal in life has that same deceptive emptiness.

The Problems of Authority

Authority has both its dangers and its limits. The Preacher knew them well, and in a loose-knit argument that covers two chapters (Eccl. 8–9) he dealt with them. The authority of the king was the theme with which he began and ended these rambling notes. And in between he touched a number of his favorite subjects which can be tied in to this discussion of authority.

The first *danger* that he saw in authority was

that it often displays *a pompousness that encourages manipulation*. The more powerful the authority is, the more it may fall victim to this. Kings were especially susceptible. Here are the Preacher's thoughts concerning them:

> Keep the king's command, and because of your sacred oath be not dismayed; go from his presence, do not delay when the matter is unpleasant, for he does whatever he pleases. For the word of the king is supreme, and who may say to him, "What are you doing?" He who obeys a command will meet no harm, and the mind of a wise man will know the time and the way. For every matter has its time and way, although man's trouble lies heavy upon him. (Eccl. 8:2–6)

We must hear the tone of this passage as well as its words. It is counsel in shrewdness; it is encouragement to cunning. Be loyal to the king—keep your sacred oath of obedience—and you will meet no harm. Furthermore, by doing this you may often get your own way, as your wisdom tells you the right time and means to gain the king's favor.

Nothing is said here about statesmanship. Nothing is said about the welfare of the land and its people. The emphasis is on the welfare of the person courting the favor of the king. "A manual on the manipulation of kings" might be the title of this section. Do what the king wants, and he will do what you want. That is the heart of the matter. We might put it even more crudely: Scratch his back, and he will scratch yours.

Unhappily, much authority works that way. The purposes for which it is given, the care with which it is to be exercised, the obligations which it carries—these are blurred when the ruler becomes heady with power. Overawed by a sense of power, such persons are vulnerable to all kinds of manipulation. Whoever will feed their pompousness by telling them how good and wise they are can readily lead them to do things that are bad and stupid.

The second *danger* that Koheleth found in authority was that it sometimes demonstrates *an arrogance that rejects limitations.* The power to wield some authority can easily be confused with the right to wield all authority. We are like office boys who sit in the boss's chair after hours and swivel ourselves in a fantasy that pictures us as masters of all we survey. Scarcely anything bubbles to the head faster than power.

Yet when it comes down to it, all authority except God's must labor under severe limitations. Our arrogance seeks to override them. But they are there nevertheless, and we use our authority best when we keep them constantly in mind.

A lesson in humility was what the wise Teacher tried to give:

> For he does not know what is to be, for who can tell him how it will be? No man has power to retain the spirit, or authority over the day of death; there is no discharge from war, nor will wickedness deliver those who are given to it. (Eccl. 8:7–8)

Let arrogance learn the limits placed on all human authority. It does not know the future and, therefore, must make its decisions humbly. It cannot stave off the day of death and, therefore, must build contingencies into its plans. It may trigger responses beyond its control, like a war, which an authority may begin but not be able to end. It may engage in wicked conduct with tragic results from which there is no recovery. Such are the pitfalls of authority when its reins are in haughty hands.

The third *danger* that Ecclesiastes noted in authority was that it often presents *a power that abuses relationships*. His summary sentence scarcely needs comment:

> All this I observed while applying my mind to all that is done under the sun, while man lords it over man to his hurt. (Eccl. 8:9)

The words are tragic: "while man lords it over man to his hurt." They can be documented in every society in every age throughout human history. The authority whose purpose is to help the human family cope with its problems and achieve its goals has been thrown into reverse gear. It has worked just the opposite of what it was intended to do. Public servants have viewed themselves as masters and laid the whip of oppression to the backs of those whom they were supposed to serve.

So it goes with authority. It is dogged with major problems. It has *dangers* which make it prone to abuse. And it has *limits* which often make its exercise ineffective. The Preacher's keen eye caught these as well.

One *limit* to effective authority is that *evil is encouraged by the delay in divine judgment:*

> Then I saw the wicked buried; they used to go in and out of the holy place, and were praised in the city where they had done such things. This also is

> vanity. Because sentence against an evil deed is not
> executed speedily, the heart of the sons of men is
> fully set to do evil. (Eccl. 8:10–11)

A profound point the preacher made. Unless people believe firmly in the reality of divine judgment, human authority has difficulty enforcing its laws. When God seems to let people get away with wrongdoing, government sanctions and strictures may prove ineffective.

Another *limit* to effective authority is that *the righteous and the wicked seem to suffer fates that they do not deserve:*

> There is a vanity which takes place on earth, that
> there are righteous men to whom it happens accord-
> ing to the deeds of the wicked, and there are wicked
> men to whom it happens according to the deeds of
> the righteous. I said that this also is vanity. (Eccl.
> 8:14)

Not only does God delay judgment, but the judgment he eventually sends sometimes seems to be backward. The wicked look as though they are being rewarded, while the cries of the righteous in distress seem to go unheeded. Authority longs to have law-breakers punished and law-abiders affirmed. But God does not always appear to cooperate.

This leads to a third *limit* to effective authority: *life seems to be governed as much by chance as by principle:*

> Again I saw that under the sun the race is not to the
> swift, nor the battle to the strong, nor bread to the
> wise, nor riches to the intelligent, nor favor to the
> men of skill; but time and chance happen to them
> all. (Eccl. 9:11)

Here again Ecclesiastes was challenging the opinions of the other wise men. Basic to their teaching was the conclusion that good conduct brought good results. Fundamental to their authority over their students was their ability to predict what would happen as the result of any course of conduct. Good causes work good effects. Speed does win the race, and strength, the battle. Diligence and intelligence do result in security and wealth. Not so, argued Koheleth. God's patterns are not predictable. Chance has at least as much influence on our well-being as human endeavor.

Still, if we have the choice between power and wisdom, we should choose wisdom. The Preacher illustrated this conclusion by the story of a wise man who was able to outwit a powerful king who attacked his city. Yet with his typically dark way of looking at life, Ecclesiastes concluded that "no one remembered that poor man" (Eccl. 9:13–15).

There we have it—a survey of the problems involved in using authority. With his usual balance, the Preacher advises us neither to grasp after it nor to rebel against it. Authority is necessary. But in our twisted, broken world, it is as much of a necessary evil as a necessary good. We need it, and we fear it at the same time. Our ambivalence was well understood by Koheleth.

The Transformation of Authority

The Preacher's response to the problems of authority was what we would expect: take pleasure where you can in a world where true pleasure is in scarce supply.

> Go, eat your bread with enjoyment, and drink your wine with a merry heart; for God has already ap-

> proved what you do.... Enjoy life with the wife
> whom you love, all the days of your vain life which
> he has given you under the sun.... (Eccl. 9:7,9)

Nothing that the Preacher said could transform our approach to authority. He helped us to keep it in perspective, but he could not set us free to follow God's path as leaders and followers; it took Jesus Christ—in whom are hid all the treasures of wisdom and knowledge—to do that.

He taught us *to be citizens without being chauvinists*. Holding aloft the coin with Caesar's inscription he offered the amazing opinion: "Render therefore to Caesar the things that are Caesar's, and to God the things that are God's" (Matt. 22:21). Without this balance, good citizenship is impossible. Only when we belong to God and his kingdom, do we know our true place in the nation whose citizenship we hold.

Because our highest allegiance is to God's authority, we are never chauvinists or narrow nationalists. We do not curry the favor of our leaders or try to manipulate them into granting special privileges. We do not overvalue them or help to enlarge their egos.

Nor do we minimize their worth. They are God's servants, called to do his will whether they know it or not. Our task is to help them know it, both by our respect for their authority and our criticism of its abuse.

Jesus taught us further *to obey the laws which God's Spirit has written in our hearts*. His Sermon on the Mount made plain that his people were subject to a spiritual authority which took them far beyond the letter of the law; lust was wrong as well as adultery;

hatred as well as murder. The inner authority is the authority of the other cheek, the second mile, the cloak as well as the coat (Matt. 5). God's Spirit within us takes us well beyond the laws of our land and binds us to the transforming authority of the law of love.

Finally, Jesus has transformed our view of authority by teaching us *to be servants in our task of leadership:*

> "You know that those who are supposed to rule over the Gentiles lord it over them, and their great men exercise authority over them. But it shall not be so among you; but whoever would be great among you must be your servant, and whoever would be first among you must be slave of all." (Mark 10:42–44)

True authority this is—not puffed up in pompousness but humbled in love, not fixed to control but bent to help.

Ambivalence there may always be in our attitude toward authority. But Jesus has given us wisdom and power to deal with it. As God's great Servant he shows us the way beyond futility, the way to authority through humility, to leadership through service.

11 / Beyond Futility —to Practicality

Ecclesiastes 10:1–20

You can hear it frequently in offices and factories around the nation. Usually it is expressed with some degree of fervor—or even anger. The context is often an occasion where a junior manager comes to his boss with a question about a difficult situation where the boss's advice is needed.

Wise supervisors resist the temptation to give advice in such circumstances. Instead they reply to the question with a statement like this: "Don't bring me problems; bring me solutions!" The point is well taken—and for several reasons, even though the spirit in which it is voiced is less gentle than it should be. The people nearest the problem usually can develop the best solutions because they know the facts intimately. Furthermore, they, not their bosses, have to carry out the suggestions. They can do this better if they have had a strong part in formulating them. Beyond that, if the supervisor has to do their thinking for them, they are not fulfilling their responsibility to him. Finally, it is obvious that pointing out a problem is normally ten times easier than discovering a solution. Identifying what is wrong in life is only a small step toward setting it straight.

Koheleth, the Preacher, was wise enough to know this. The management maxim—solutions, not just problems—was familiar to him.

Though he is best known for the sharp way in which he pointed out the false values to which his countrymen had dedicated themselves, he should also be remembered for the practical solutions that he gave to many human problems.

Most notable is the theme that sounds prominently through his book, whenever he pauses in his negative statements to give a bit of positive counsel. Perhaps the fullest statement of it is this:

> Go, eat your bread with enjoyment, and drink your wine with a merry heart; for God has already approved what you do. Let your garments be always white; let not oil be lacking on your head. Enjoy life with the wife whom you love.... Whatever your hand finds to do, do it with your might.... (Eccl. 9:7–10)

High and heady pleasures he has condemned as a chief goal in life. Realism in facing death he has strongly advocated. Yet here, simple pleasures and homey joy are what he wants his students to treasure. Satisfying basic wants, living in warm fellowship, making the best of a difficult life—these are his abiding values.

He was not a hedonist. Pleasure was an entrapping snare, not an alluring idol. Disciplined enjoyment, not wild carousing was his great goal in life.

His call to modest enjoyment was grounded in his belief in practical conduct. Despite all his questionings and criticisms, he was at heart a wise man, a teacher of sound behavior. Frequently, this concern for practical wisdom bobs to the surface, especially in the latter chapters of his book. Solutions as well as problems were what he contributed to his time—and ours.

Let Wisdom be Your Guide

In his earlier chapters he warned us not to bank on wisdom as life's highest good:

> For in much wisdom is much vexation,
>   and he who increases knowledge increases
>   sorrow. (Eccl. 1:18)

He was speaking to extremists, to those who touted wisdom as the key to life's problems, as the pearl of great price for which everything else should be sold. He warned those who praised wisdom to the heavens that it would produce at least as much pain as blessing.

He made his misgivings clear about those who overvalue wisdom. Yet nowhere did he celebrate folly. With all its problems, wisdom was to be heartily preferred to folly. Do not let wisdom be your god, but let it be your guide, was his advice.

Foolishness has its dangers, and the Preacher warned his pupils against them:

> Dead flies make the perfumer's ointment give off an
>   evil odor;
>   so a little folly outweighs wisdom and honor.
>   (Eccl. 10:1)

Folly has dangers and wisdom has limits—those twin points are made in that proverb. Folly is so powerful that a little of it—like a bad smell—can overwhelm large amounts of wisdom.

Folly is also dangerous because it heads us in the wrong direction:

> A wise man's heart inclines him toward the right,
> but a fool's heart toward the left. (Eccl. 10:2)

With apologies to left-handed people, we must note that *left*, here, is synonymous with evil. And this evil inclination cannot be hidden. Folly has a way of betraying itself:

> Even when the fool walks on the road, he lacks
> sense,
> and he says to every one that he is a fool. (Eccl.
> 10:3)

Folly has its dangers, and *wisdom has its advantages*. Ecclesiastes used two proverbs to make this clear:

> If the iron is blunt, and one does not whet the edge,
> he must put forth more strength;
> but wisdom helps one to succeed. (Eccl. 10:10)

And,

> If the serpent bites before it is charmed,
> there is no advantage in a charmer. (Eccl. 10:11)

"An ounce of prevention is worth a pound of cure" would probably be our English equivalent, or "a stitch in time saves nine." Wisdom helps us save energy—like the wisdom to sharpen the axe ahead of time. Wisdom prevents accidents—like the foresight to charm the snake *before* it bites. Simple, practical wisdom to keep our folly from showing itself and hurting us—that was the wise Teacher's aim in this chapter.

Wisdom is a guide in *governmental affairs*. That was a point that Koheleth returned to frequently. Like all wise men he recognized that human life is basically political. Whether we thrive or chafe will in large measure depend on how we are governed. All of us— from tribal aborigines to urban intellectuals—live under governments. Knowing how to deal with those who order and regulate our lives is an essential part of our education.

The Preacher's advice was practical—almost shrewd: "stay on good terms with the powerful." Two proverbs sounded that signal:

> If the anger of the ruler rises against you, do not
> leave your place,
> for deference will make amends for great offenses.
> (Eccl. 10:4)

Do not run from your mistakes even when they anger the ruler. Let your calmness and gentleness turn his anger aside. Even more, think positive thoughts about the leaders of the land, even in private,

> for a bird of the air will carry your voice,
> or some winged creature tell the matter. (Eccl.
> 10:20)

Discretion is a virtue, for rich and powerful people often have ways of finding out who their enemies are. Rumor and gossip can fly like birds.

"Be aware of life's injustices" was another part of his practical advice. The sharp eye of the preacher had seen rulers make tragic mistakes. They had often put the wrong people in power:

> folly is set in many high places, and the rich [and
> therefore wise] sit in a low place. (Eccl. 10:6)

The warning is a good one. Inequities do arise in life, especially in government. But the Preacher did not tell us what to do about them. Are we to correct such abuses or merely to be warned against them? In his kind of society, there may not have been much choice.

What counted was the quality of the leadership. "Rejoice in good government" was his strong counsel. Immature leadership, especially leadership that indulges itself in carousing, is a woe to any people. In contrast,

> Happy are you, O land, when your king is the son
> of free men,
> and your princes feast at the proper time,
> for strength, and not for drunkenness! (Eccl.
> 10:17)

Our society is indeed fortunate. Most of us have the power not only to rejoice in good government but to change bad government or governors where necessary. Drunkenness and folly in high places are not what we have to put up with. We can best show our respect for governmental authority by insisting that it keep its contracts and fulfill its responsibilities with efficiency and integrity.

Let wisdom be your guide in government affairs, and in *personal matters* as well. "Do not harm your neighbor" was one of the guidelines of wisdom. The Teacher used a series of interesting proverbs to warn of the dangers of harsh or rash conduct toward others. Our attacks on others boomerang on us. The aggressor ends up with the most grievous wounds:

> He who digs a pit will fall into it;
> and a serpent will bite him who breaks through a
> wall.

> He who quarries stones is hurt by them;
>> and he who splits logs is endangered by them.
>>> (Eccl. 10:8–9)

A pattern of retribution is built into the structure of life. Those who make hurting others their aim hurt largely themselves.

"Control your tongue" was another wise guideline:

> The words of a wise man's mouth win him favor,
>> but the lips of a fool consume him. (Eccl. 10:12)

Gentle and moderate talk can accomplish infinitely more than the endless babble of fools.

"Find enjoyment through work" was the last bit of personal counsel. Both security—like making sure the roof does not leak—and pleasure—like the joy of bread and wine—depend on work and the money it produces (Eccl. 10:18–19).

Let Love be Your Aim

Jesus, too, believed that God's people should have the wisdom to deal with life's problems. When he commissioned his disciples, he gave them this advice: "Behold, I send you out as sheep in the midst of wolves; so be wise as serpents and innocent as doves" (Matt. 10:16). That is about as practical as one can get—counseling persons to guard against persecution without becoming bitter or hostile.

In what ways did Jesus lead his people beyond the shrewd advice of Koheleth? How did he show himself as the greater Wise Man? He gave us *a firmer confidence in God*. Ecclesiastes set out patterns for his pupils to follow; Jesus introduced us to the person of his Father. The older wise man wanted his students to understand how life worked; the greater Wise Man called his followers to know the One who makes life work. Practicality at its best—this knowledge.

Jesus also brought to us *a clearer awareness of God's kingdom*. This active, personal rule of God among the human family was a major theme of his ministry. To his disciples he issued these orders: "And preach as you go, saying, 'The kingdom of heaven is at hand.' Heal the sick, raise the dead, cleanse lepers, cast out demons. You received without pay, give without pay" (Matt. 10:7–8). "The kingdom of heaven is at hand"—what practical words these are! God is at work in our world, in our history, in our society, in our lives. His power to save and to heal, to comfort and to convict is at hand. His demands become our guide, and his provisions, our resources. What an older wise man could only *encourage* us to do, the power of God's Spirit *enables* the citizens of the kingdom to carry out.

This awareness of God's kingdom also taught us how to deal with human government—a theme to which Ecclesiastes gave more than passing attention. God's kingdom requires us to be citizens responsible to our earthly governments, while it also insists that our first loyalty is to the Lord who created us and redeemed us. We respect our governors but we do not fear them. They, too, with all their pomp and power, are subject to God's authority. They govern best when they govern according to his will; we serve our governments best when we encourage them to do this.

Finally, Jesus took his pupils beyond the wisdom of the older Preacher when he instilled in them *a stronger sense of the power of love.* So much of what Ecclesiastes said dealt with shrewd conduct. Jesus knew that getting along in life was more a matter of concern than cunning. He spurred his disciples to pray for their enemies and to do good to those who mistreated them. Make love your aim—not just success. Make love your aim because love *is* success—by God's measurements. Those were Jesus' exhortations. He who knew God's ways perfectly because he himself was God knew that God's ways are the ways of love.

The wisest, most practical solution of all was what Jesus brought. When we remember all the pain caused when we are clever but not compassionate, when we are shrewd but not generous, when we are sharp but not sensitive, we can vouch for the practicality of love. Solutions, not problems, are what we need. Like no one else in history, Jesus met our need.

12 / Beyond Futility
—to Fruitfulness

Ecclesiastes 11:1–10

Ours may be the first generation in civilized times that has not raised its young on proverbs. From the beginnings of recorded history in Egypt and Sumeria, concise sayings which describe the benefit of good conduct or the harm of bad have been used to teach children how to behave.

From the islands of the sea to China, from the Bedouin of the Arabian peninsula to the Eskimos of Alaska, proverbs have been a standard way of summarizing life's experiences. In our own country both the biblical proverbs of Solomon and the Anglo-Saxon wisdom collected in Poor Richard's Almanac by Benjamin Franklin have helped generations of parents coach their children in the art of successful living.

Because proverbs are based on experience, they work best in situations where change is non-existent or gradual. Settled, rural societies where the pattern of life has remained much the same for centuries find proverbs a congenial way to package and pass on their wisdom. Tribal life, with its uniformly accepted values and its stable social relationships, usually employs a rich stock of proverbs.

Our generation—for the most part—has abandoned the use of proverbs, although one still finds them on locker room walls. There loud signs exhort athletes to do their best with slogans like "When the going gets tough, the tough get going," or "What matters is not the win nor loss but how you play the game." Proverbs have seemed too preachy for many of our young people. They have sought to discover their own values rather than to conserve the values of the past. Change has been such a constant companion in their lives that they have discarded yesterday's wisdom in a frantic effort to cope with a future that seems so different from the past.

But perhaps the old saying is proving true, "The more things change, the more they stay the same." Proverbs seem to be coming back into vogue. From bumper stickers to wall posters, from embroidered hangings to desk mottoes we see wisdom placarding its advice. Once again we may begin to raise our youngsters with warnings to caution like, "Look before you leap," or to decisiveness like "He who hesitates is lost." When they chafe under our advice, we may remind them of these words:

> Poverty and disgrace come to him who ignores instruction,
> but he who heeds reproof is honored. (Prov. 13:18)

A world burned and scarred by new values that proved false, or a world confused and bitter at the absence of values much needed may well turn to proverbs to regain its sense of direction. Proverbs—wise sayings which capture the lessons of experience and bring some order to the chaos of living—are one of the means that men and women have used to deal with the seeming futility of life.

Even Ecclesiastes, who spoke so much of life's futility when people tried to make profit or pleasure or prestige or permanence their aim, used proverbs to help his students make their way beyond the futility, beyond the vanity, he so forcefully described. How to be fruitful in a world where so many lives are barren was one question that he handled with proverbs.

Make the Most of What You Have

Fruitfulness, as the Preacher defined it, meant both prosperity and joy. Having things was not enough, if a person could not enjoy what he had.

Make the most of what you have, counseled the wise man, and you will find *the path to prosperity*. His first proverb that illustrated this is familiar yet misunderstood:

> Cast your bread upon the waters,
>   for you will find it after many days. (Eccl. 11:1)

Our misunderstanding is that we usually take this casting of bread as a picture of charity. "Do good deeds and you will be rewarded" is our customary interpretation.

But the Preacher's practical shrewdness and the context within the book suggest something else—namely, advice not about charity but about wise investment. Where did one gain the highest return on his money? In investments overseas; in the rich export and import business of the Mediterranean ports like Tyre and Sidon. Bread upon the waters that you will find after many days was Ecclesiastes' way of describ-

ing investment in those lucrative mercantile enter-
prises where fortunes were to be made.

There was risk involved, of course. And the
Teacher urged his students to diversify their investments to hedge against such risk:

> Give a portion to seven, or even to eight,
>   for you know not what evil may happen on earth.
>   (Eccl. 11:2)

Misfortune and calamity (here called "evil") are part of
life. Who knows what crop will fail, what ship will be
seized by coastal pirates, what merchant will abscond
with the profits? Spread your investments widely—to
seven or eight places—so that no one or two tragedies
can wipe you out. That advice was part of the path to
prosperity.

Hard work as well as wise investment was
what the Preacher prescribed as part of his formula for
fruitfulness. Apparently some of his countrymen were
paying too much attention to the actions of the wind
and the clouds—not as observers of the weather, but
as practicers of magic. They believed that the climate
had to be just right for them to do their work success-
fully, especially their sowing and reaping.

Leave all that to God, Koheleth commanded.
He will do his work on schedule, even if you do not
understand it.

> If the clouds are full of rain,
>   they empty themselves on the earth;
> and if a tree falls to the south or to the north,
>   in the place where the tree falls, there it will lie.
>   (Eccl. 11:3)

The processes of creation go on without your worry,

and you could not change them if you tried. So get on with your work, Ecclesiastes urged.

Too much contemplation of the right time or the suitable season may mean that no work is accomplished:

> He who observes the wind will not sow;
> and he who regards the clouds will not reap.
>   (Eccl. 11:4)

Overcaution causes a lack of nerve that freezes us into inactivity. That was what the Preacher warned against.

He also warned his pupils not to try to guess God's ways. They are as mysterious as the act of conception:

> As you do not know how the spirit comes to the bones in the womb of a woman with child, so you do not know the work of God who makes everything. (Eccl. 11:5)

Let God take care of his mysteries and you take care of your work, was his conclusion:

> In the morning sow your seed, and at evening withhold not your hand; for you do not know which will prosper, this or that, or whether both alike will be good. (Eccl. 11:6)

Make the most of what you have—that has been the gist of Koheleth's teaching to his students who long to find the path to prosperity in a world marked by so much futility. But what good is prosperity where there is not the power to enjoy it? Grim prosperity is only slightly better than dark poverty. Joy is an essential ingredient if we are to do more than survive.

So alongside the path to prosperity, the wise Preacher lined out *the road to joy*. Find the beauty in every day, was his simple advice:

> Light is sweet, and it is pleasant for the eyes to behold the sun. (Eccl. 11:7)

At the beginning of his book, Ecclesiastes had called attention to the wearisome futility with which the sun made its daily round (Eccl. 1:5). Here his outlook is different. Reminded of life's fragility, he encouraged his friends to celebrate every hour of daylight.

There is an urgency to this celebration, noted the wise Professor, because *death is coming* and lasts so long:

> For if a man lives many years, let him rejoice in them all; but let him remember that the days of darkness will be many. All that comes is vanity. (Eccl. 11:8)

Enjoy the tasks at hand; savor each bit of food and drink; share your joys with the wife of your youth. Make the most of what you have, Ecclesiastes has urged, because the days of darkness are coming when your enjoyment will cease. Death will pull the blinds and black out the lights of life.

God is judging how well you celebrate his gifts. That is the last of Koheleth's counsel on the road to joy:

> Rejoice, O young man, in your youth, and let your heart cheer you in the days of your youth; walk in the ways of your heart and the sight of your eyes. But know that for all these things God will bring you into judgment. Remove vexation from your mind, and put away pain from your body; for youth and the dawn of life are vanity. (Eccl. 11:9–10)

Vanity here means fleeting, brief. Like a bubble the days of our youth soon burst, so we have to clutch them while we can. Obviously the wise man was not counseling a rebellious or wild style of life when he told his students to "walk in the ways of your heart." Lawlessness, wickedness, lewdness, were as much out of bounds for him as for any of Israel's wise men. Take your fill of life; do your best at what you do; live each day to the hilt in work, in love, and in the enjoyment of God's good gifts. All of these are displays of God's grace; he will judge us as to whether we have made the most of them.

Be the Best at What You Are

Most of this Old Testament advice has been affirmed by the New Testament's greater Wise Man. He, too, believed that we should make the most of what we have. This was part of what he had in mind in his parable of the talents. Who can forget his stinging words:

> "Then you ought to have invested my money with the bankers, and at my coming I should have received what was my own with interest. So take the talent from him, and give it to him who has the ten talents. For to every one who has will more be given, and he will have abundance; but from him who has not, even what he has will be taken away." (Matt. 25:27–29)

Abilities, goods, wealth, opportunities—all these are divine gifts of which we are stewards. One of the things that Jesus will do when he comes again is to judge how well we have used his gifts.

Part of our commitment to Jesus as Lord is our

commitment to invest our money, our time, our energy in endeavors that will pay dividends. Ecclesiastes was right. But he did not tell the whole story. He did not know that the coming of our Lord Jesus is the event toward which all our living and giving and saving and spending point. If God-fearing men and women in Old Testament days felt that wisdom demanded sound investment of what they had, how much more should we, as Christ's return approaches?

And part of our commitment to Jesus as Lord is to rejoice in God's good gifts. In the heart of the prayer that the Master taught his followers is the plea for daily bread. What Jesus urged us to plead for, God has promised to supply. Though we do not live on bread alone, we do need bread for the sustenance and refreshment of life. Our Savior made wine at a wedding and celebrated in advance that great Wedding yet to come, by eating and drinking with crooked tax collectors and known sinners.

In doing this he taught us a greater enjoyment, a higher prosperity, than Koheleth's friends could imagine. Jesus taught us to eat and drink in enjoyment of God's provision; but more than that he taught us to eat and drink in anticipation of God's victory. The day is coming when all of God's people will sit at history's finest banquet and will feast to the full in fellowship with each other and with the Savior, who is our Bridegroom. Every Christian meal, every Christian party, every gathering in Christian fellowship should be enlivened with the hope of the Banquet yet to come.

Jesus wants us to make the most of what we have in the use of our goods and the enjoyment of his gifts. But beyond that, he wants us to be the best at what we are. What are we basically? Investors? Yes, and hopefully wise ones. What are we? Enjoyers? Yes, and preferably grateful ones.

Yet we are more. We are *lovers*, meant to adore God's person and to serve our neighbor's needs. These are the human realities, the spiritual yearnings, that Ecclesiastes saw only dimly.

In Jesus they come clear. What he says to us takes us beyond all futility to full fruitfulness: "I am the vine, you are the branches. He who abides in me, and I in him, he it is that bears much fruit . . ." (John 15:5).

Love is the fruit on which Jesus focused: "This is my commandment, that you love one another as I have loved you" (John 15:12). To many, proverbs and slogans may seem an obsolete method of teaching the way to success. This command can never be obsolete. It is rooted in the very nature of God; it flowered in the sacrifice of Jesus Christ; it is the true source of human fruitfulness. Where love is at work, there is no room for futility, for "love never ends" (I Cor. 13:8).

13 / Beyond Futility —to Maturity

Ecclesiastes 12:1–14

He was a theologian, a teacher, and a mountain climber. I knew that, but I was still not ready for his words: "I would like to get another crack at the Alps or at least a chance to tackle the Tetons." His eyes were steely as he spoke, and they flashed with hopes about the future.

Speechless in amazement, I looked at his lithe, tall frame, trim as a javelin, erect as a lance. My amazement was not based on any doubts about his prowess. His climbing feats were known to a wide circle of his acquaintances. What surprised me about his hopeful words of scaling the Alps or the Tetons was the fact that he was over ninety years of age.

He knew what it was to grow older without letting either the thought or the reality of aging destroy his spirit. In so doing he had learned one of life's most needed lessons. He had learned to mature while he aged. His spirit had enlarged and ripened even while his body felt the taxing toll of time. Joy and hope were strong even where muscles and sinews had begun to weaken.

Coping with the futility that some feel in old age was a skill he had developed well. His vitality defied the grotesque picture of aging that Ecclesiastes' skeptical brush had sketched at the close of his book. His last words were inked with anxiety over a foreboding future. Do you suppose it was his own aging that he dreaded? Like the rest of us preachers, were his sharpest words directed at himself? Was he raising the volume of his voice to calm his own fears?

Take Life's Pleasures Now

> Remember also your Creator in the days of your youth, before the evil days come, and the years draw nigh, when you will say, "I have no pleasure in them." (Eccl. 12:1)

This was not a command to piety so much as to pleasure. The Preacher was not begging his pupils to get right with God in terms of obedience, but of enjoyment. Bad days are coming in which pleasure will be impossible, was his warning. Take life's pleasures now. Remember your Creator—remember that God has given you his gifts for your pleasure. Make the most of them while you have the energy and the vitality, was his exhortation.

In light of the aging process, take life's pleasure now. Nowhere in Scripture are the ravages of old age described more brutally than in Ecclesiastes. "Evil days" he has called them, days fraught with misfortune or even disaster.

He embellished this description with three unforgettable word pictures. Old age is like the coming of winter, was his first and most gentle comparison:

> Remember also your Creator . . . before the sun and
> the light and the moon and the stars are darkened
> and the clouds return after the rain. (Eccl. 12:1–2)

Most of the year in the Bible lands the sun could be
counted on every day. But in winter, after the autumn
rains, cloudy, colder days would come. These were
the days when nature was dormant—the days between the rich fall harvest of fruit and grapes and the
appearance of the almond blossoms as the messengers
of spring. Leafless trees, songless birds, fruitless
vines, clouded skies—these were the signs of winter.
And they were also symbols of the barren, desiccated
life of old age, when pains were many and pleasures
few.

His next and fullest picture compared old age
to the collapse of a mighty household. Its details are so
many and so vivid that they have to be studied one by
one. Hard times are ahead, he has warned, "in the day
when the keepers of the house tremble, and the strong
men are bent" (Eccl. 12:3)—in the day when our arms
and legs are too shaky and weak to do their full work.
Other members of the body will also find their powers
fading: "and the grinders cease because they are few,
and those that look through the windows are dimmed,
and the doors on the street are shut" (Eccl. 12:3–4).
Loose or missing teeth ("the grinders"), cataract-cov-
ered eyes, and deaf ears ("doors . . . shut") are part of
the price that age exacts. Aging may also make us
anxious so that we speak in low tones and jump at any
strange sound. The Preacher described this as a time
"when the sound of the grinding [i.e. conversation] is
low, and one rises up at the voice of the bird [or any
startling sound]" (Eccl. 12:4). And on top of this our
voices begin to crack and a firm, steady tone becomes

harder to maintain: "and all the daughters of song are brought low" (Eccl. 12:4). The level of fear is apt to rise—fear of high places and fear of terror in the streets (Eccl. 12:5)—two experiences to which older people are still vulnerable.

The final picture of aging likened the elderly to almond trees in blossom—crowned with white hair—and to a dragging grasshopper—fragile of limb, unable to walk without crutch or cane (Eccl. 12:5). Perhaps the most poignant phrase in the catalog of woes is this: "and desire fails" (Eccl. 12:5). To the Preacher who prized life's simple enjoyments—work, food, drink, love—the failing of desire meant the loss of what he deemed good. Therefore, he urged his young students to "remember also your Creator," who has given us good things to enjoy and the youthful power to enjoy them.

Age is marked not only by the curtailment of pleasure but by the imminence of death. *In view of pending death*, take life's pleasures now. The Preacher used brilliant poetic imagery to embellish that command. He described death as the loss of light and water—two essentials of life in Palestine or anywhere else. The light fails when the silver cord that holds the lamp breaks and the golden bowl that contains the oil burned by the lamp is broken. The water is lost when the pitcher used to draw water from the well is smashed or the wheel which scoops up water from the cistern ceases to work.

These poetic figures are interpreted by words familiar to us from the story of creation in Genesis:

> and the dust returns to the earth as it was, and the spirit returns to God who gave it. (Eccl. 12:7)

In other words, Ecclesiastes saw death as the reversal of creation. But there was no joy to this picture. The return of the human spirit to God he did not see as a triumphal entry to the courts of heaven. The whole process of aging and the fearful imminence of death were the last stages of a life scarred by futility. And the Preacher ended his words as he had begun them twelve chapters earlier:

> Vanity of vanities, says the Preacher; all is vanity.
> (Eccl. 12:8)

He did not tell us what he believed about the return of the human spirit to God, but his tone indicated that it was not an experience worth looking forward to.

Part of what Koheleth the Preacher dreaded, modern technology has cared for. Good nutrition has slowed the aging process for millions, while sound dental care, simple eye surgery, miniature hearing aids all help to surmount physical deterioration. Not to mention the way hair dressers can deal with the white "almonds" that thatch our heads!

But the fact that we work so hard to keep young—and sometimes more important—to look young, shows how accurately the wise man perceived our human problem. Our life expectancy has increased, and we are able to keep our vitality longer, yet for all of us the silver cord does snap and send the lamp of light crashing; the pitcher and the wheel do break and the water of life is spilled. How do we keep those realities from writing "futility of futilities" like grim graffiti on our fences?

The wisest man of his time could not help us much with that question. The person—perhaps one of his students—who preserved Ecclesiastes' words for us gave his teacher high marks:

> Besides being wise, the Preacher also taught the people knowledge, weighing and studying and arranging proverbs with great care. The Preacher sought to find pleasing words, and uprightly he wrote words of truth. (Eccl. 12:9–10)

Yet despite the wisdom, the care, the truthfulness with which he did his work, our wise Teacher could do little more than to help his students face life's—and death's—realities. He did all that could be expected of a wise man in collecting knowledge and conveying it. He gave his students words to depend on, words that ultimately came from God—the source of all true wisdom:

> The sayings of the wise are like goads, and like nails firmly fixed are the collected sayings which are given by one Shepherd. (Eccl. 12:11)

And he summarized all he had said about making the best of life's simple pleasures and allowing God the freedom to be mysterious in these words:

> The end of the matter; all has been heard. Fear God, and keep his commandments; for this is the whole duty of man. For God will bring every deed into judgment, with every secret thing, whether good or evil. (Eccl. 12:13–14)

Fearing God and keeping his commandments must be understood in the light of what the Preacher has been saying throughout the book. God's will, he has told us, is that we not build our lives on wisdom, wealth, prestige, or lust. Rather, we should accept life as it is with its problems and mysteries and savor its modest pleasures as we can. To do this is to fear God and obey him. Grasping after more, or chafing because we have less, is futile. God reserves to himself the right to determine our lot; our response is to make the best of it. That is why Koheleth's theme from beginning to end is "take life's pleasures now."

Look Forward to Your Destiny

The Christian gospel has better news to offer than the somber analysis of the old Preacher. And it has a better prescription for our geriatric problems. "Take life's pleasure now" was a maxim that the early Christians would have understood, though they would have added other ingredients to Ecclesiastes' recipe— ingredients like enjoying Christ's fellowship and witnessing to his kingdom. But "take life's pleasure now" cannot be the only advice the gospel gives, if it is to be good news. What good will it do us to seize *today* if we dread *tomorrow* with its creeping senility and its looming death.

The better prescription that Jesus Christ offered was this: "Look forward to your destiny." What Koheleth had said was to live all you can while you can, because the time was coming when such exuberant life would be impossible. What Jesus said was to live fully all your life, even in old age—and beyond.

Doing God's will was part of what Jesus ordered as a way of maturing and not just aging. *Aging* is a negative process. It speaks of wrinkles and trembles, of frosted vision and spotty hearing. *Maturing* is a positive experience. It points to greater wisdom and increased patience, to stronger love and enriched understanding.

One great purpose of the Christian gospel is to help us grow as persons into a maturity patterned after Christ's. *Doing the will of God* is central to this growth.

It is the heart of our relationship with God, a relationship that refines and mellows us, that strengthens and perfects—in spite of the limitations of aging. Is this not what Jesus meant when he pointed to his disciples and said, "Here are my mother and my brothers! For whoever does the will of my Father in heaven is my brother, and sister, and mother" (Matt. 12:49–50)?

Doing God's will means living in his love and centering on his purposes. It brings us into line with him and with ourselves. It keeps us alert and hopeful because it presents us with fresh possibilities. At times we may feel like lame grasshoppers, but opportunities for love are ever present, and strength to love is not totally dependent on physical vitality. The aged are good at loving, especially when they have matured for decades in the knowledge that God loves them.

Facing death with confidence was another part of Jesus' prescription for maturity. The specter of death is part of what makes old age a wintry season. Jesus urged his followers not to fear it even when it came in violent forms. Their attention was to be given to God, not to those who might bring about their death: "And do not fear those who kill the body but cannot kill the soul; rather fear him who can destroy both soul and body in hell" (Matt. 10:28). The God who notes the fall of the sparrow cares much about his own children. He will see us through the door of death and beyond. Beyond the door where the lamp has been broken and the pitcher has been smashed is brighter light and sweeter water. Our dying is his business; his will is our business. The aged are good at trusting, especially when they have matured for decades in their confidence that God cares.

Moving in history's direction was a third part of

Jesus' pattern for maturity. Time marches on, but not by itself. God is moving it as part of his program that began at creation and will consummate with Christ's coming. The passing of the years is not a scourge but a sacrament. It is God's way of heading history in his direction. If time seems to be taking its toll, if your household seems to be short of staff, remember that Jesus pointed his life toward that *hour* when he would glorify God and rescue us by his death. We can let time do its work, even though it sometimes seems cruel, with the hope that time's work is God's work. It is heading not so much toward death as toward life. The aged are good at hoping, especially when they have matured for decades in the truth of the promises of God.

Look forward to your destiny. It may not be climbing the Alps or the Grand Tetons in your nineties; it may be something far grander and more adventuresome—like doing God's will in love and trust, facing death with courage and confidence, and moving in history's direction with hope and anticipation. Aging may have its futile sides, but its futility is no match for the maturity that Christ provides.

Conclusion

By now the wise Preacher has made his point: most of what we lean on to bring meaning and dignity to our lives will burst like a bubble under our weight. We have to make the best of an awkward situation in which things cannot be depended on, and God is not always available. What God gives we are to use, without expecting any more than the simple gifts of work to do, food to eat, and friends to love.

These creations of God offer more profit than all the more promising lures which compete for our attention. Two millennia and more have not proved the wise man wrong. Our modern quest to make sense of life has the same frenetic foolishness to it that the Preacher censured. The options which he discarded, we are still pursuing. His words about their vanity, their futility, are timely.

We need to heed them—and more. We need to hear the Master Sage, the Wiser than Solomon, sent by the Father with the keys to life in his hands. All interim solutions can be set aside. The fullness of truth has stood in our midst, given the lie to our errors, and pronounced passé all temporary solutions.

Ecclesiastes tried to lead his pupils beyond the futility of their fellows, but he also warned them not to go further than where he had taken them:

> My son, beware of anything beyond these. Of making many books there is no end, and much study is a weariness of the flesh. (Eccl. 12:12)

Perhaps we would have obeyed the Preacher, if something else had not happened. Not another book, but a final Word. A Word that called all of us to find in study not weariness but rest: "... learn from me; for I am gentle and lowly in heart, and you will find rest for your souls" (Matt. 11:29). It is his students, his disciples, numbering now in the scores of millions, who have learned to move beyond futility—far beyond.